SECRET PROVIDENCE

A GUIDE TO THE WEIRD, WONDERFUL, AND OBSCURE

Rebecca Keister

Copyright © 2017, Reedy Press, LLC
All rights reserved.
Reedy Press
PO Box 5131
St. Louis, MO 63139
www.reedypress.com

No part of this publication may be reproduced or transmitted in any form or by any means, electronic or mechanical, including photocopy, recording, or any information storage and retrieval system, without permission in writing from the publisher. Permissions may be sought directly from Reedy Press at the above mailing address or via our website at www.reedypress.com.

Library of Congress Control Number: 2017934676

ISBN: 9781681061061

Design by Jill Halpin

All photo credits belong to author unless otherwise noted.

Insert Image Credits:
   Backstage Gallery: Providence Performing Arts Center
   Barnaby's Castle: Christian Scully
   Dragon Races: James Toomey for Blackstone Valley Tourism Council
   Extra, Extra Innings: PawSox
   Industrial Invention: James Toomey for Blackstone Valley Tourism Council
   Necronomicon: Necronomicon Providence
   Purgatory Chasm: Paul Irish, https://www.flickr.com/photos/paul_irish/159463161
   Revere Bell: Richard Boober Photography
   Rose Island Light: Kate Grasso Photography
   Touro Synagogue: Swampyank via Wikimedia Commons
   Vroom, Vroom: Audrain Car Museum

Printed in the United States of America
17 18 19 20 21   5 4 3 2 1

DEDICATION

To Michael, Adam, and Patrick, my beloved brothers, for all their support and guidance.

CONTENTS

1	Introduction
2	Big Blue Bug
4	*Gun Totem*
6	Anthropodermic Books at Brown
8	Sideburns Forever
10	Roger Williams Tree Root
12	Rhode Island Red
14	Hope
16	Extra, Extra Innings
18	All the Doughnuts
20	Superman!
22	What Cheer
24	Floating History
26	Rhode Island's Sistine Chapel
28	Stuffies
30	Gaggers
32	The Providence Flea
34	Good Boy, Hachiko
36	Barnaby's Castle
38	Rose Island Lighthouse
40	Dragon Races
42	Musée Patamécanique
44	Vroom, Vroom
46	Vampire Grave
48	Axe That
50	Backstage Gallery
52	Unbeneficial Provenance
54	Factory of Fantastic Finds
56	Irish Lot

58	Stuck-Up Bridge
60	Highpointing Fix
62	Spring Lake Arcade
64	Presidential Portrait
66	We'll Drink to That—Rhode Island's Refusal to Ratify Prohibition
68	Flying Horse Carousel
70	Industrial Invention
72	Cogswell Tower
74	Seabee Museum
76	Big Nazo Puppets
78	Johnny Cakes
80	Museum of Work and Culture
82	Favorite Toys
84	Doyle's Haunting Grounds
86	Fleur-de-Lys Studios
106	Jailhouse Inn
108	Providence Biltmore Hotel
110	Great Swamp Fight Monument
112	The Palatine Light
114	White Horse Tavern
116	Beatrice's Room
118	Revere Bell
120	U-Pick 'Em
122	Neutaconkanut Hill
124	St. Mary's Church
126	Purgatory Chasm
128	Ladd School
130	Rose Ferron's Grave
132	V-J Day
134	Bristol Fourth of July Parade
136	Touro Synagogue

138	NecronomiCon
140	Temple to Music
142	Fort Adams
144	Southernmost School House
146	Carey Mansion
148	Fort Wetherill
150	Carrie and the Count
152	Blue Violet
154	Stephen Hopkins
156	Cumberlandite
158	An Epic Food Fight
160	Swan Point Cemetery
162	Narragansett Rune Stone
164	Coffee Milk
166	Birth of the American Diner
168	Green Animals Topiary Garden
170	Southeast Light
172	Brown & Hopkins Country Store
174	Newport Tower
176	H. P. Lovecraft
178	Little Bet
180	Rhode Island's Plymouth Rock
182	JFK Grave Slab
184	You're a Grand Ol' Rhode Islander
186	Elizabeth Alden Grave
188	Weird Laws
190	Nine Men's Misery
192	Tennis, Anyone?
194	Stuck in a Gun
196	Index

INTRODUCTION

It all started with a simple greeting, an iteration of which is still used today. When Providence founder Roger Williams landed here in 1636, having fled Massachusetts for fear of religious persecution and prosecution, he was greeted by Rhode Island's native Narragansett tribe, whose chief held up a hand and said, "What cheer, Netop?" In today's words, this is loosely translated as "Hi, friend, how goes it?" And so, the city's and state's reputation as a welcoming solace for the freethinking, independent, and adventurous was formed. That sentiment is still present across Rhode Island today in its culture, its people, and the preservation of its historic charm. It's no surprise then that the roadside oddities, attractions, and places of worship and rest across the state have some surprising secrets that answer questions many have never thought to ask. Why are there life-size monsters at times roaming downtown streets? How did the state come to be the only one with an official appetizer? Where was baseball's longest-ever game played? Is a former mayor forever trapped inside a city hall, haunting its workers? Where can I climb to the highest point in the city and the state? Why is there a muzzled cannon on display at the state house? Welcome to *Secret Providence*, a guide to the city's and state's weird, wonderful, and obscure places, people, and attractions, which are waiting to be explored. This collection is meant to introduce you to the unusual and little known, to provide you with insider information about your favorite places, and to encourage additional investigation into your favorite things about Providence and Rhode Island. Whether you're visiting for the first time or rediscovering the creative capital, this guide will give you a lens into the beautifully unusual, the somewhat sad, the hauntingly historical, and the uniquely traditional.

1 BIG BLUE BUG

Where can you see the world's largest "insect"?

Several landmarks can be found along Route 95 that announce motorists' arrival to or departure from Providence, but since 1980 none has been more famous than Nibbles Woodaway, the Big Blue Bug. At 58 feet long and 9 feet tall, Nibbles (named in a 1990 contest), the 4,000-pound mascot of pest control company Big Blue Bug Solutions, is an exact replica of the Eastern subterranean termite and watches over travelers from its perch atop the company's roof. Constructed out of wire mesh and fiberglass, the mascot was originally purple to be the same color as a live termite, but its hue changed to blue under sunlight, and as its reputation as the "Big Blue Bug" grew, the company decided to keep the new shade. Now quite the celebrity, Nibbles has made appearances on national shows, including the *TODAY* show and *The Oprah Winfrey Show* and has been seen in several movies, including *Dumb and Dumber*. Come holidays, Nibbles can be seen dressed for the occasion, sporting a witch's hat around Halloween and clad in stars and stripes for the Fourth of July, but Christmas is his big season to shine, and there's even an annual lighting ceremony to debut a Rudolph-themed costume each year.

For your own safety, don't try to take this bug's photo!

Nibbles Woodaway, the mascot for Big Blue Bug Solutions, keeps watch over travelers on Route 95 in Providence. Photo courtesy of Richard Kizirian Photography

NIBBLES WOODAWAY

WHAT Big Blue Bug Solutions mascot, a roadside attraction

WHERE Route 95 in Providence

COST None

2 GUN TOTEM

Why are 1,000 guns fossilized in the city?

It's been called a roadside attraction on many a bucket list, but the *Gun Totem* outside Providence's federal courthouse is much more. In 2001, the Providence Parks Department commissioned Rhode Island-based metal-working artist Boris Bally to design and construct an installation at the Convergence, an international arts festival that was a predecessor to today's PVDFest. The result is a city point of pride, a beautiful example of an artist's unique vision and a sober reminder of both the dangers of gun violence and the fact that it only takes a few individuals with a vision to make a difference. Bally constructed the *Gun Totem* with 1,000 used handguns from Goods for Guns, a firearm buyback program founded by Dr. Michael Hirsh, a pediatric surgeon and medical school professor, in Allegheny County, Pennsylvania. He has since expanded the program to the Northeast. Bally had collaborated with Hirsh in 1997 to create a touring art show from disassembled guns that were collected and turned in by owners in exchange for gift cards one Christmas season. When the Providence commission came in, Bally embedded 1,000 of those guns—which normally would be demolished by a metalsmith—in steel and cement to create the fossilized effect of the 14-foot obelisk that was meant to stand just for a brief time but has remained in the city in part because moving it proved too difficult. To date, Goods for Guns has collected more than 11,000 guns.

GUN TOTEM

WHAT Local artist Boris Bally's installation, a pillar composed of 1,000 guns collected from a firearm buyback program based in Pennsylvania

WHERE Across from the Providence County Courthouse's South Main Street entrance.

COST None

The Gun Totem is an installation of 1,000 fossilized guns outside Providence's Federal Building and U.S. Courthouse created from fire arms collected during a buyback program.

Given the installation's sensitive nature, some explanation might be needed before visiting with children.

3 ANTHROPODERMIC BOOKS AT BROWN

Why does Brown University house volumes bound in human skin?

It's something anyone except writers of horror fiction would find repulsive today, but centuries ago anthropodermic bibliopegy—the practice of binding books in human skin—was considered an acceptable if not preferable way to fasten published works. Scholars most widely estimate that the practice began in the mid-16th century and lasted through sometime in the 19th century and is known to have been conducted by doctors who had access to their patients' skin. It is also reported that some volumes were bound by wealthy book collectors and that skin for the books regularly came from criminals or the very poor. Some editions were even made from the skin of people who requested it upon their death. Brown University's John Hay Library has four books certified as anthropodermic books, including a 1568 anatomy text and two editions of the *The Dance of Death*, printed in the 19th century. As is the case with other libraries that house anthropodermic books, including the Boston Athenaeum in Boston, the books at Brown University are only available for viewing to scholars conducting research. In addition to the books being extremely rare, librarians and curators are ethically bound not to display such works for everyday observation.

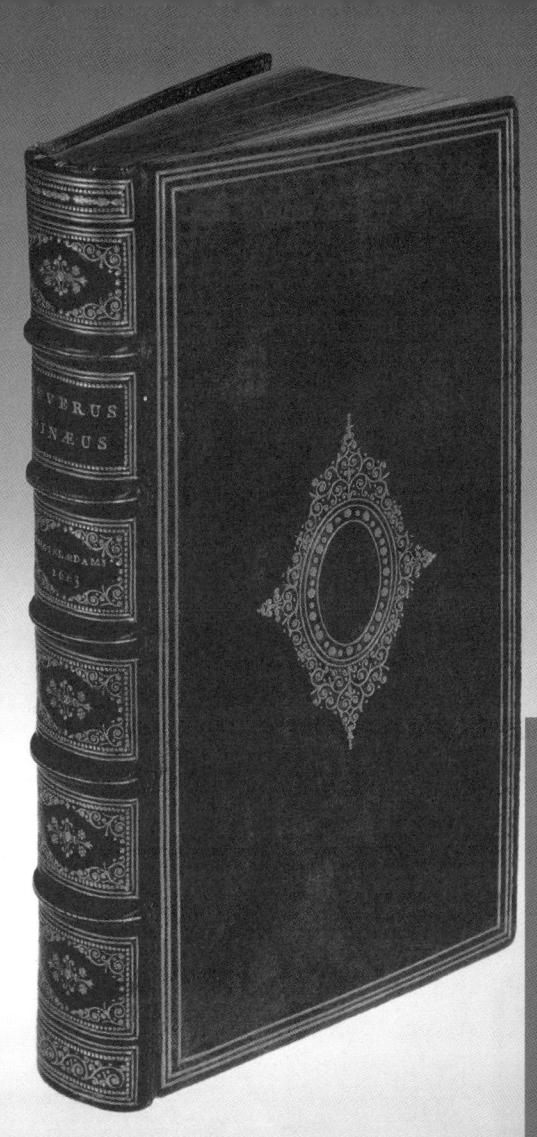

Brown University, the state's Ivy League school, houses a few books bound in human skin, like the one seen here from a London library. Photo courtesy Wellcome Images via Wikipedia Commons

ANTHROPODERMIC BOOK COLLECTION AT BROWN UNIVERSITY

WHAT Four books bound in human skin

WHERE 20 Prospect St., Providence

COST The books are made available for scholarly research

Human skin-bound books look just like leather-bound books; the difference is in the texture, which is akin to a bumpy suede feel.

4 SIDEBURNS FOREVER

Where can you pay homage to the father of sideburns?

He might not have invented them, but former Rhode Island Governor Ambrose Burnside (1866–1869), who was a general in the Union army during the U.S. Civil War, made sideburns what they are today—at least in name. Though sideburns reportedly have been an on-and-off grooming style since 100 B.C., Ambrose Burnside became infamous during his military career for what others deemed his "unusual" habit of growing out his moustache and letting his side whiskers grow long so that the two appeared connected while leaving his chin clean shaven. The style became known as burnsides, and somewhere along the pop culture trajectory, the name morphed into sideburns. The Civil War was certainly not the last time the style was in fashion. From hippies to hipsters and metrosexual rebels, men throughout modern history have embraced this distinctively defining style. A statue of him on horseback, which is located in Providence's Burnside Park (adjacent to Kennedy Plaza downtown), was erected in his honor in the late 19th century, providing sideburn fans for generations to come the opportunity to pay their respects to the style's namesake.

Governor Burnside is buried in Swan Point Cemetery at 585 Blackstone Boulevard, another spot to pay homage to sideburns.

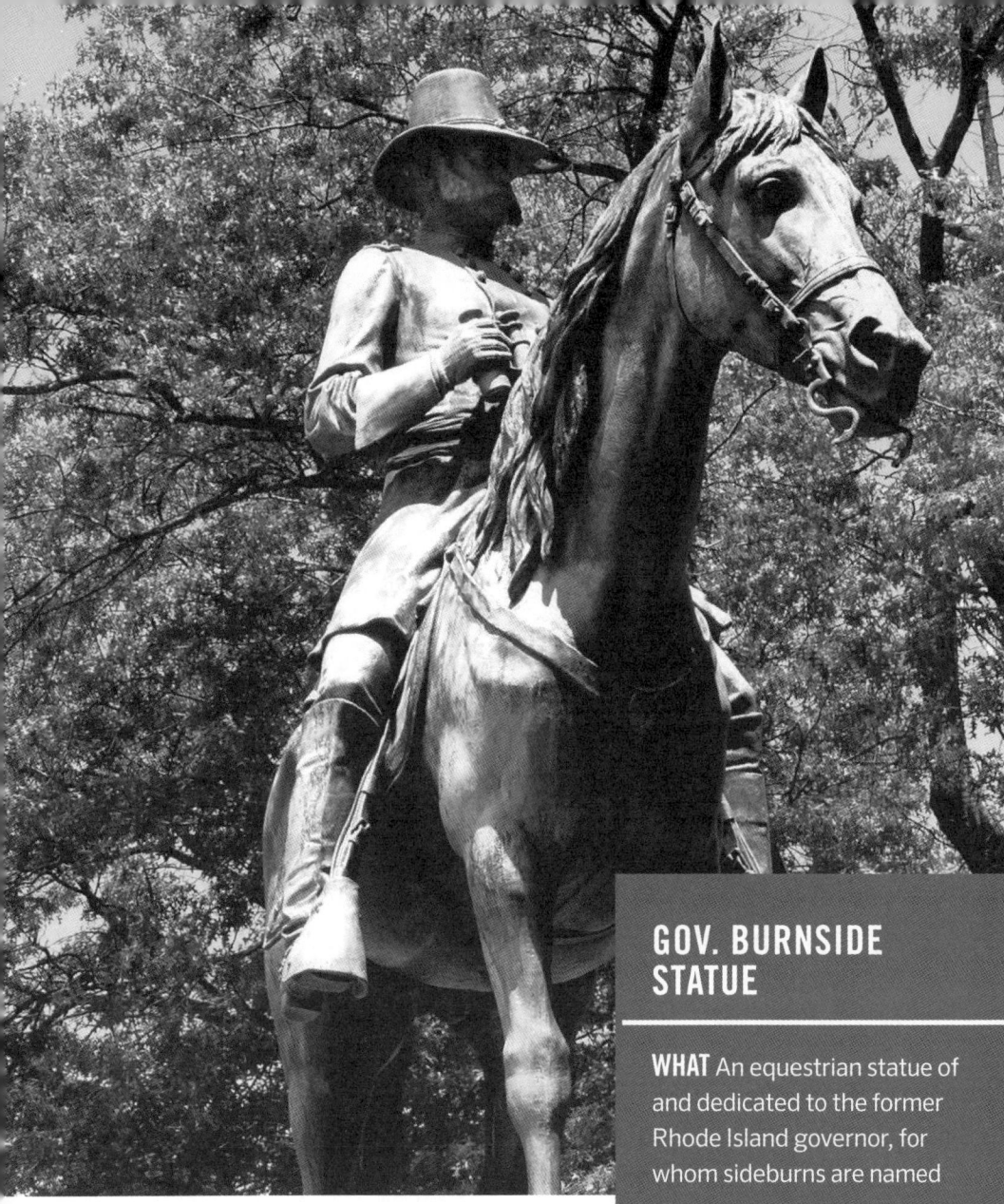

Those favoring the sideburns look can thank former Rhode Island Governor Ambrose Burnside for the style, or at least for its name. Photo by Hal Jespersen via Wikimedia Commons

GOV. BURNSIDE STATUE

WHAT An equestrian statue of and dedicated to the former Rhode Island governor, for whom sideburns are named

WHERE Burnside Park, 2 Kennedy Plaza, Providence

COST None

5 ROGER WILLIAMS TREE ROOT

Did an apple tree really eat Rhode Island's founder?

The scenario's very unlikely validity hasn't stopped observers of oddity and hunters of myth from embracing speculation that the buried body of state founder Roger Williams was eaten by the root of an apple tree. About 200 years after his death, a group of community leaders in 1860 retrieved what they assumed to be his remains to include in a planned memorial, but their excavation also turned up an apple tree root that they—and many others throughout the years—felt had taken the form of his body. Because the root was shaped like a body—including a branching off that resembles two legs and upturned feet—and because excavators found evidence of remains but not an entire corpse, they declared that an apple tree root must have found its way around and inside his coffin and devoured him. No scientific evidence proves this speculation, but that hasn't stopped locals, historical theorists, and embracers of the weird, wonderful, and obscure from holding onto the idea. To accommodate the curious, the Rhode Island Historical Society agreed to house and display the root—inside a coffin-shaped frame—and visitors to the John Brown House Museum can see it there.

History buffs can visit Williams's memorial at Prospect Terrace Park, at the corner of Congdon and Cushing Streets in the city's College Hill neighborhood.

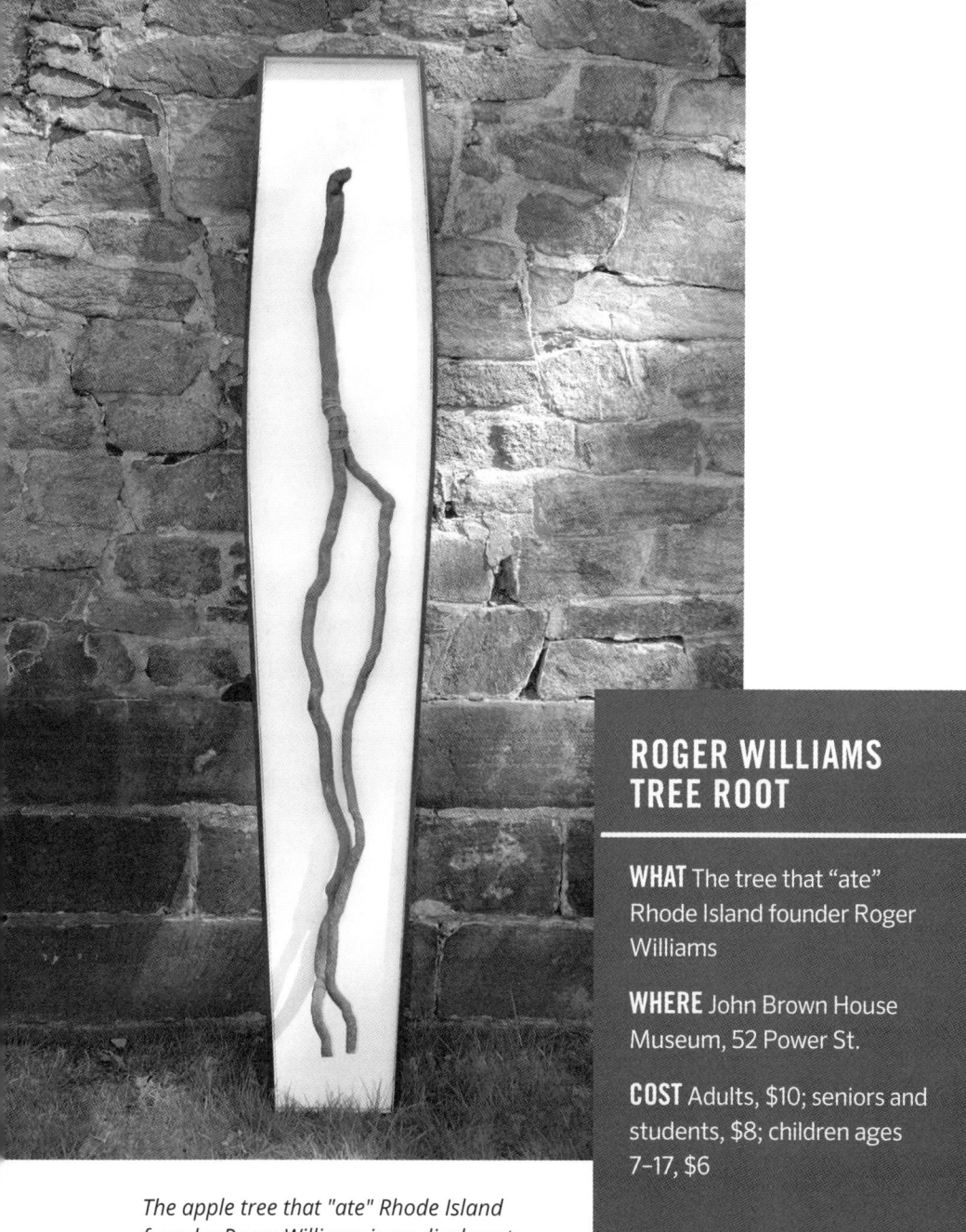

The apple tree that "ate" Rhode Island founder Roger Williams is on display at the John Brown House Museum. Photo courtesy of the Rhode Island Historical Society Collections

ROGER WILLIAMS TREE ROOT

WHAT The tree that "ate" Rhode Island founder Roger Williams

WHERE John Brown House Museum, 52 Power St.

COST Adults, $10; seniors and students, $8; children ages 7–17, $6

6 RHODE ISLAND RED

How did Rhode Island come to have a chicken as its state bird?

The very short answer to this question: in a contest. In 1954, the Audubon Society of Rhode Island—along with the Rhode Island Federation of Garden Clubs and the Providence Journal Company—held a contest to name a state bird. The Rhode Island Red was the winner, and Governor Dennis J. Roberts signed the choice into law on May 3, 1954. The bigger story is that Rhode Islanders engineered the chicken, and the state served as its original breeding site. The Rhode Island Red is a domestic chicken created in the late 1800s through cross-breeding, making it one of three state birds that are not native to the United States. Who can claim naming rights to the chicken is debated. Some sources point to a Rhode Islander and some to a Massachusetts poultry farmer, but it's documented that the bird was first bred in Adamsville, a village in the quiet town of Little Compton. The bird is so beloved that two monuments are dedicated to it in Rhode Island. The first, which is on the National Register of Historic Places, was funded by the Rhode Island Red Club of America in 1925 and is located in Adamsville. The second, erected in 1988, is dedicated to the farmers who grew Rhode Island Reds in Little Compton.

Visitors will find Rhode Island Red emblems and associations on a variety of souvenirs to take home.

The Rhode Island Red, the state's official bird, was created here through cross-breeding. Photo courtesy of Vitag via Wikimedia Commons

The bird is so popular, two monuments stand in its honor. Photo courtesy of Swampyank via Wikimedia Commons

RHODE ISLAND RED MONUMENT

WHAT National Register of Historic Places monument dedicated to Rhode Island's state bird

WHERE Intersection of Adamsville Rd., Westport Harbor Rd., and Main St. in Adamsville

COST None

7 HOPE

Why Rhode Islanders live off hope

Hope. It's one word that packs a lot of punch, and in Rhode Island, where it's more than just a mantra, it is invoked to look toward a better tomorrow. Here, it's the state motto—truly the word to live by—or, as the saying here goes, hope is what to live off. The state motto officially dates to 1896, when the General Assembly's adoption of the Rhode Island arms of the state, or state emblems, became effective, but several reports point to colonists adopting a seal with the word hope included as far back as the 1660s. Within the state emblems law is included "the motto thereof is the word 'Hope.'" The word is written above an anchor that has served as a symbol of Rhode Island since Colonial days, and it is thought, according to historical notes printed in 1930, that the word and symbol were selected from the biblical phrase "hope we have as an anchor of the soul." Some residents *literally* live on Hope, as several streets throughout the state are named after the state motto. The state is a place where ". . . most of us live off Hope"—the motto coined by longtime resident and artist Mad Peck and immortalized in a poster he created in the late 1970s, versions of which can be found in local souvenir shops.

In Rhode Island, most of us live off Hope, the state motto.

HOPE

WHAT Rhode Island's state motto

WHERE Hope Street is on the city's East Side

COST None

Hope Street is one of the best spots for shopping and dining, with a variety of boutiques and eateries to suit every taste.

8 EXTRA, EXTRA INNINGS

Where was the longest-ever baseball game played?

Spectators at the April 18, 1981, Triple-A International League game between the Pawtucket Red Sox and the Rochester Red Wings had little idea that they were settling into a seat in history that night at McCoy Stadium. When the game was finally over—with 32 innings played over April 18 and 19 and the last inning taking place two months later on June 23—the two teams would play for eight hours and 25 minutes across 33 innings with the PawSox victorious 3-2. So, what happened? The attending umpire's rule book did not contain a reference to the league's curfew rule that would have suspended the game at 12:50 a.m. When the ninth inning ended 1-1, the teams played on and on, until 4:07 a.m. the next day with a tie score of 2-2 after players started reporting they were near collapse from exhaustion. (The game had tied a second time in the 21st inning.) By that point, only 19 fans were left in the stands. For their dedication, they were given season or lifetime passes to McCoy Stadium. When the Red Wings next visited Pawtucket, it was to a sellout crowd of 5,746 and 140 reporters from around the world. The game lasted just 18 more minutes before Pawtucket's Dave Koza scored the winning run. A ball signed by both teams is on display at the Baseball Hall of Fame in Cooperstown, New York, and in 2006 the PawSox celebrated the 25th anniversary of the game with several events, including a luncheon attended by the Red Wings.

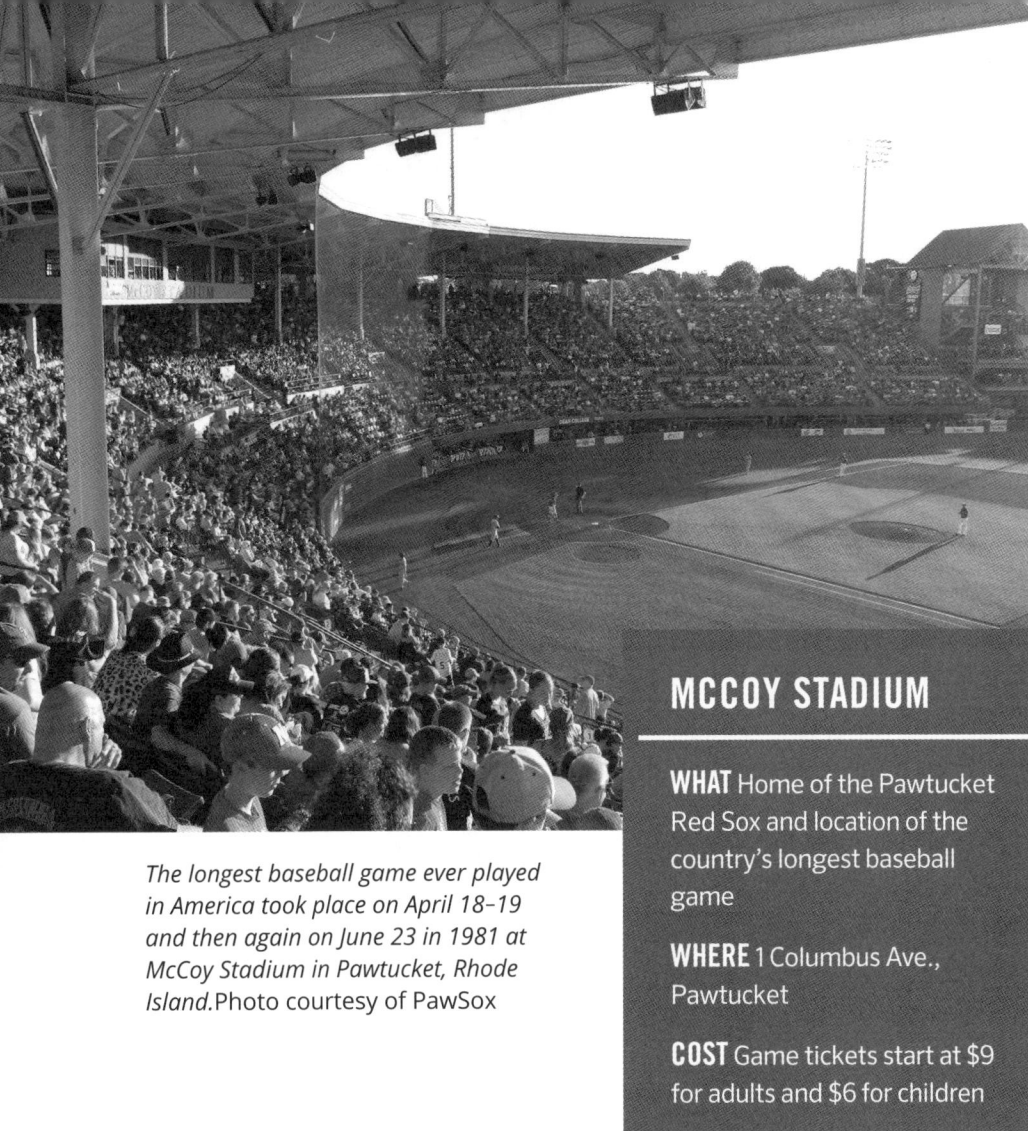

The longest baseball game ever played in America took place on April 18–19 and then again on June 23 in 1981 at McCoy Stadium in Pawtucket, Rhode Island. Photo courtesy of PawSox

MCCOY STADIUM

WHAT Home of the Pawtucket Red Sox and location of the country's longest baseball game

WHERE 1 Columbus Ave., Pawtucket

COST Game tickets start at $9 for adults and $6 for children

Take the children out for a good, old-fashioned ballgame. This park is very family friendly, and games feature regular appearances by Paws and Sox, the team's mascots. Many games also conclude with a dazzling fireworks display.

9 ALL THE DOUGHNUTS

Why is Providence the best place for this sugary breakfast confection?

Some claims to fame—being a place that is the *capital* of something—are a self-proclamation born out of a reputation for having the best of that something. But regarding doughnuts, Providence has serious bragging rights. Twice within the last decade—in 2010 and 2014—food industry market resource firm NPD Group has confirmed that the Providence metropolitan area has the most doughnut shops per capita of any area in the United States. It should be noted, though, that contributing to this distinction is a great number of Dunkin' Donuts shops, franchises of the Massachusetts-headquartered chain—not to disparage the company's popularity in Rhode Island, which is quite high. However, independent, artisanal shops offering one-of-a-kind doughnuts are just as greatly appreciated here for their sometimes quirky and often delicious treats. In 2017, Tastemade, a food-and-travel video network, named Allie's Donuts—a North Kingstown shop famous for its doughnut cakes—the third-best doughnut shop in the country, adding to its best-of list wins. PVDonuts, a city shop that specializes in locally sourced confections, offers a rotating menu of specialty brioche doughnuts that has gained national attention for such creations as a doughnut topped with an entire Thanksgiving dinner. And that's just two of the area's shops. No matter how you like them—crafty or cream filled—the country's doughnut capital has something for every taste.

PVDonuts, in the city's Fox Point neighborhood, is an artisinal doughnut shop attracting doughnut lovers to line up for daily specials.

DOUGHNUTS

WHAT Providence has been named the U.S. doughnut capital several times for having more doughnut shops per capita than any other national region, though the title has gone to other areas—including Boston—some years. In 2014, the area had 25.3 doughnut shops per 100,000 people.

WHERE Various locations

COST Depends on the doughnut shop

PVDonuts, an artisanal shop on the East Side, regularly attracts an around-the-corner line and is known to sell out of daily treats well before closing time. It's best to get there early for your a.m. sugar fix.

10 SUPERMAN!

What's the real story behind the city's most well-known building?

Look! It's a skyscraper! It's an architectural landmark! It looks like the building in the *Superman* TV show! Providence's "Superman Building"—its official name is the Industrial Trust Building—is all of this and more. Perhaps Rhode Island's most recognizable building, it's the tallest in Providence—at 428 feet high—and the 28th tallest in New England. Constructed in the late 1920s in the Art Deco style, it was opened to tenants as the Industrial Trust Tower in 1928 when Providence, like many major cities, was enjoying a postwar economic boom. For the next 84 years, its aesthetic prominence and host of financial tenants became a symbol of prosperity and then hope for the city until 2012, when its last tenant closed shop. Since then it's remained empty and a source of contention and speculation on what's best for its future. This isn't so different from the tall tales that have surrounded the building over the years that, despite being widely refuted, have added to the building's allure. Among these is that the building served as a landing spot for zeppelins—large German airships that took on commercial travelers post-World War I—and that the building was the inspiration for the Daily Planet building in the 1950s *Superman* TV show. Although the resemblance is noticeable, and the nickname stuck, Los Angeles City Hall is actually shown on the program. Pop culture experts are correct in identifying the "Superman Building" in skyline shots on TV's *The Family Guy,* created by Rhode Island native Seth MacFarlane.

INDUSTRIAL TRUST BUILDING

WHAT Providence's most iconic piece of architecture, once a shining symbol of the state's prosperity, now with an uncertain future

WHERE 111 Westminster St., Providence

COST None

The Industrial Trust Tower, better known locally as the Superman Building, is an iconic part of Providence's downtown skyline. Photo courtesy of Kenneth C. Zirkel via Wikimedia Commons

The Providence Preservation Society has started giving tours of the building. When tickets go on sale, catch them fast—they've been known to sell out within hours.

11 WHAT CHEER

How did Providence get its motto?

As for mottos, Providence's "What Cheer"—sometimes written with a "?" at the end—is one of the country's oldest and one of Rhode Island's most revered, with a backstory that pays tribute to the ideals and values upon which the city and state were founded. As the tale goes, as Rhode Island founder Roger Williams was fleeing Massachusetts in 1636 to escape religious persecution, he canoed across the Seekonk River, and upon reaching land was greeted by a tribe of Narragansett Indians who called out, "What cheer, Netop?" an informal greeting of the times shortened from "What cheery news do you bring?" and likened today to something like, "Hey! What's up?" Williams went on to negotiate acquisition of the land he came upon in an agreement that allowed the Narragansetts access to English trade goods. Besides a spot on the city seal, you'll also find it on a variety of keepsakes in artsy stores throughout the city. The state's craft beer pride and joy, Narragansett Beer, has incorporated it into their slogan of "Hi, Neighbor!" using the English translation of "Netop," and several businesses, artists, and buildings over the years have used "What cheer" in their naming. It's a motto that speaks to the city's reputation as that of a welcoming, tolerant people and to their appreciation for a founder who wasn't afraid to create his own paradise.

The Narragansett Beer logo is one iteration of Rhode Island's state motto, "What Cheer!?" which loosely translates to "Hi, neighbor!" Photo courtesy of Narragansett Brewery

WHAT CHEER

WHAT City of Providence motto

WHERE N/A

COST None

Visiting the newly reestablished Narragansett Brewery and greeting those gathered with a "Hi, Neighbor!" will earn you some local cred.

12 FLOATING HISTORY

Where can you spend a night on America's only operating British canal boat?

Rhode Island's Blackstone River, which flows for 48 miles between Rhode Island and Massachusetts, was named for William Blackstone, the first European to put down roots in what is now Boston and who was important in the development of America's Industrial Revolution in the late 18th century. Today, it is largely a beautiful backdrop for recreational adventures, including walking, biking and cruising, and—perhaps most impressively—is home to the *Samuel Slater,* this country's only authentic operating British canal boat, the kind that used to travel frequently up and down the river from 1828 to 1848. The Blackstone Valley Tourism Council commissioned the boat in 2000 as part of its Millennium Project, and it was constructed in Cambridgeshire, England. The 40-foot *Samuel Slater* offers the adventurous traveler accommodations on a floating bed-and-breakfast and can host up to four people for an overnight stay. Equipped with a full working kitchen, hot-shower bathroom, electricity, and Wi-Fi, it is described as an ideal choice for those wanting to experience a little bit of English history and culture without crossing international waters. While overnighters can add a river cruise to their experience, complete with the chance to steer the ship, the *Samuel Slater* is also available for charters or small parties.

Overnight stays are bookable through Airbnb.

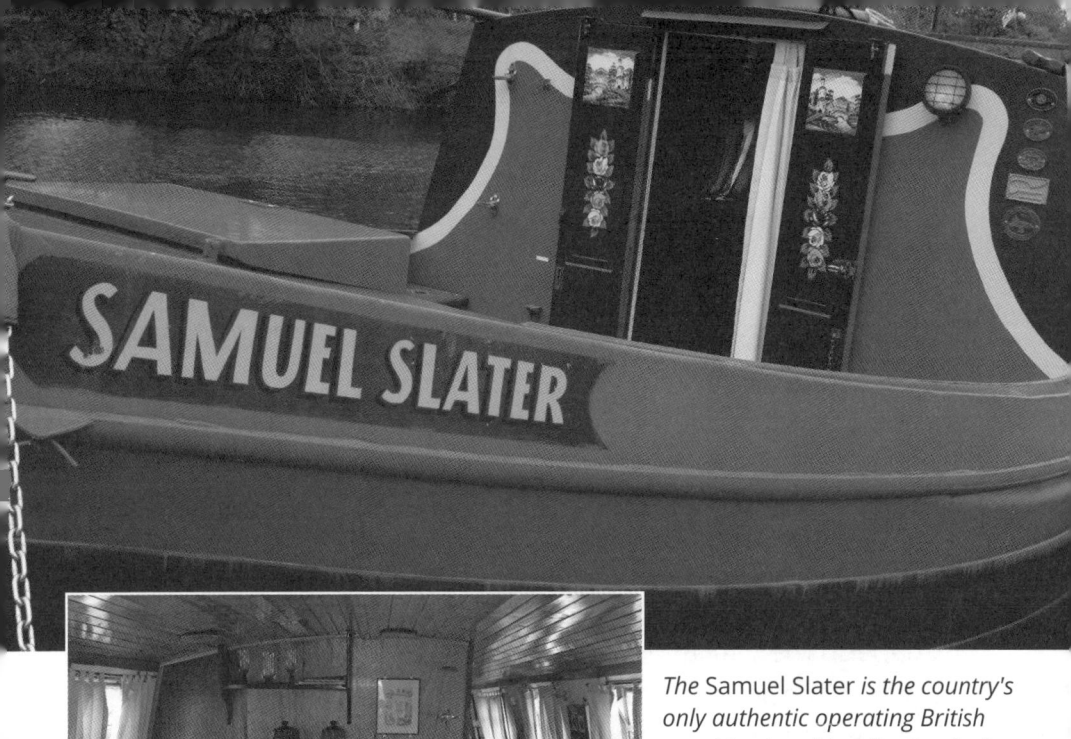

The Samuel Slater *is the country's only authentic operating British canal boat and is a floating bed-and-breakfast docked in Central Falls, Rhode Island.* Photo courtesy of James Toomey, Blackstone Valley Tourism Council

Guests on the Samuel Slater *enjoy a full working kitchen.* Photo courtesy of James Toomey, Blackstone Valley Tourism Council

THE *SAMUEL SLATER*

WHAT The United States' only authentic operating British canal boat and a floating bed-and-breakfast

WHERE Central Falls Landing, corner of Broad St. and Madeira Ave., Central Falls

COST $185 overnight stay for two people; $20 for each additional person up to four total. Charter cruises are $250 for 90 minutes

13 RHODE ISLAND'S SISTINE CHAPEL

Where can you see the Northeast's largest collection of fresco paintings?

After immigrating to Montreal, Canada, in 1915, Italian-born artist Guido Nincheri (1885–1973) made his mark in North America by decorating churches across Canada and New England with stained glass windows and fresco paintings. Fresco—perhaps most well known for adorning the Sistine Chapel in the Vatican—is a technique of mural painting in which the artist paints on fresh or wet lime plaster, using water to help pigment move with the plaster and creating the effect that the mural is etched into or is part of the wall on which it is painted. In the 1940s, St. Anne's Cultural Center—then an operating Catholic Church—commissioned Nincheri to adorn its walls, vaults, and ceilings with fresco paintings, and the painter used parish members as his models when he created what remains the largest collection of fresco paintings in North America. Built between 1913 and 1917 by the French-Canadian immigrants who flocked to Woonsocket during the birth of America's Industrial Revolution, St. Anne's was closed and sold by the Catholic diocese in 2000. Luckily, former parishioners, conservationists, and fans banded together and incorporated the former church into a nonprofit organization that today is run exclusively by volunteers and serves as a valuable cultural offering to all of Rhode Island. Nincheri's work can be seen in several other Rhode Island churches and buildings, including the Church of Christ the King in West Warwick and the Roger Williams Park Museum of Natural History and Planetarium in Providence.

The largest collection of fresco paintings in North America is housed at St. Anne's Cultural Center in Woonsocket. Photo courtesy of St. Anne's Cultural Center

ST. ANNE'S CULTURAL CENTER

WHAT St. Anne's Cultural Center, home to North America's largest collection of fresco paintings

WHERE 84 Cumberland St., Woonsocket

COST Tours are general admission, $10; seniors & students, $8; children ages 4 and under, free

Tours are 1:00 p.m. to 4:00 p.m. on Sundays, but the center is closed during the winter months.

14 STUFFIES

How did the quahog come to be Rhode Island's state shell, and just what is a stuffie?

What exactly is a quahog, pronounced ko-hog? Rhode Islanders will often be asked this question when the topic of local-only food comes up. They'll also often be asked if it is in fact a real city here, and the answer to this is that *Family Guy* creator and Rhode Island native Seth MacFarlane very cleverly made it up. A quahog is a large, hard clam native to waters off the eastern shores of North America and Central America. Its name is a variant of "poquauhock," the Native American name given to the clam. On June 30, 1987, Rhode Island adopted the quahog as its state shell as an ode to its longtime importance to both the state's fishermen, who can catch the clam year-round, and Rhode Island residents, who have long enjoyed quahogging (clam digging) as a leisure activity. Quahogs can be used in any recipe or dish that calls for clams, but the most treasured here is the stuffie, which, at its most basic, is a breadcrumb-and-minced-clam mixture that is served on the quahog half-shell. You'll often find a stuffie packed with much more than that and most often with chorizo, the Spanish sausage. Recipes vary by restaurant, and you're likely to get a different recommendation from almost every person you ask. This dish may be available at eateries outside Rhode Island, but make no mistake: it's a Rhode Island dish and is so synonymous with the state that it was featured as one of the must-tries on a 2016 episode of *Bizarre Foods with Andrew Zimmern* on the Travel Channel titled "Rhode Island: Chowing Gaggers & Stuffies."

The quahog, from which stuffies are made and on which they are served, is the state shell.

STUFFIES

WHAT A Rhode Island seafood tradition; a clam designated as Rhode Island's official state shell

WHERE Various locations

COST Depends on the restaurant

In 2016, the Rhode Island Department of Environmental Management—in partnership with several other state entities, local organizations, and restaurants—began hosting a springtime Quahog Week, with dining specials and events planned around the clam and celebrating the state's seafood industry.

15 GAGGERS

Why do Rhode Islanders eat something with such a name?

Speaking of gaggers . . . Those not in the know may scoff at the idea of trying—let alone loving—a food with what is perhaps an unappetizing moniker, but "gagger" is another local term for a hot wiener, one of the state's most beloved culinary traditions. Fans and fans-to-be can thank the Stevens family, which owns and operates two Olneyville New York System restaurants in Rhode Island and has been serving up their unique recipe since the 1930s. The Stevens family got their start running a candy shop in Brooklyn, New York, during the 1920s after emigrating from Greece. Make no mistake: this is not a hot dog—nor is it ever called one—and ketchup is not the condiment of choice when indulging. That's because it's dressed with mustard, meat sauce, celery salt, and onions and then served up in a steamed bun. The real secret is the family's unique sauce, made with a signature blend of six spices and available to take home so that you can try making your own—just make sure to use the recommended 80 percent (or less) ground beef. Truthfully, though, you'll want to enjoy them at the restaurant, which won a 2014 James Beard Foundation America's Classic Award honoring it as an eatery with "timeless appeal" and "beloved for quality of food that reflects the character of their community," where the family has been serving Rhode Island's "original fast food favorite for over 60 years."

GAGGERS

WHAT Another name for hot wieners, a Rhode Island hot dog served with a local-only sauce

WHERE For the best, Olneyville New York System, 18 Plainfield St., Providence

COST Under $4 for two wieners and a soft drink

Be sure to order your gaggers "all the way" or with the works.

If you truly want to feel like a local, walk up the counter and order two wieners "all the way"—that's with all the fixings.

16 THE PROVIDENCE FLEA

How did one woman's idea for a unique side business transform into a must-visit city shopping fair?

Rhode Islander Maria Tocco's idea was relatively simple. Take the successful working model of "funky flea markets" found in Brooklyn, New York, and transplant it to the state's creative capital, set up shop in the heart of the city where views of the architecturally significant skyline might impress, fill it with one-of-a-kind crafts made by talented artisans and, for good measure, have food trucks at the ready to whet the appetites of hungry shoppers. The verdict? In just a few short years, The Providence Flea has gone from idea to inspiration. Though its creator remains a bit modest about her success, her idea to create a juried vintage and maker market that would not only bring together fellow entrepreneurs but also foster relationships between them and the greater community has more than come to fruition. What's more, it has created a dialogue around the possibility that her model could be replicated to enhance the state's creative economy. In short order, it's the city's best-kept shopping secret and one that is invested in the city's betterment. The Flea features a local nonprofit each week and has collaborated with other organizations to build a tighter community.

The Flea is held on Sundays. Visit one of the city's unbelievable brunch spots, do some shopping, and then grab a food truck snack for an authentically local experience.

The Providence Flea is the city's best-kept shopping secret, offering both the chance to peruse locally crafted goods and enjoy an afternoon out on Providence's water front. Photo courtesy of Providence Flea

THE PROVIDENCE FLEA

WHAT Unique organization of vendors and entrepreneurs coming together for a pop-up marketplace full of good wares and good times

WHERE Winter and spring as well as holiday markets are held in the Hope High School cafeteria, 324 Hope St., Providence. Summer markets are held on the Providence River Greenway across from 345 South Water St., Providence. Fall market locations are announced yearly

COST Depends on the vendor and your food truck appetite

17 GOOD BOY, HACHIKO

Where can you see a tribute to the most revered dog in Japanese history?

A long time ago (1925) in a place far away (Japan), a golden-brown Akita known as Hachiko captured the hearts of commuters using the Shibuya Station in Tokyo. Following the sudden death of his owner, Hachiko continued to greet the afternoon train daily as he had always done for another nine years, nine months, and 15 days (until his own death). Folks brought Hachiko treats and food, and local newsmen and authors published stories about the dog's daily trek. Hachiko became an emblem of national loyalty and fidelity, and since the 1930s, a bronze statue erected in his honor has become a popular meeting spot for locals, commuters, and tourists. Hachiko's reputation went international in the 2011 film *Hachi: A Dog's Tale*, which starred Richard Gere and was filmed in various locations around Providence and neighboring Woonsocket, with the latter city's train depot serving as the train station. In 2012, the City of Woonsocket installed a replica of the bronze Hachiko statue—given as a "token of appreciation and loyalty to the city"—at the train depot during that year's Rhode Island Cherry Blossom Festival to honor the spot as a filming location and to enhance the city's support of expanding Japanese culture in Rhode Island.

Woonsocket's Hachiko statue pays tribute both to the most revered canine in Japanese history and the major motion picture that was filmed in this town. Photo courtesy of the Blackstone Valley Heritage Corridor

HACHIKO STATUE

WHAT A statue installed as a tribute to the legend of Hachiko, a Japanese symbol of loyalty and fidelity

WHERE Woonsocket Train Depot, 1 Depot Square, Woonsocket

COST None

Enhance your experience by first watching the 2011 film, with tissues, since it is a tearjerker.

18 BARNABY'S CASTLE

Where can you tour a castle in the city?

He may have made a name for himself as a 19th-century clothing magnate, but Jerothmul Bowers Barnaby's legacy is best embodied in his glorious High Victorian mansion located in the heart of the city's West Side. Barnaby built his mansion, a two-and-a-half-story building, with the help of Rhode Island architectural firm Stone, Carpenter & Willson, in 1875, though the four-story, 12-sided tower on its left side and round conservatory near the front were added in 1885. Named by some as the best-known Providence house from its era, the mansion features among other elaborate elements a mansard roof (characterized by increasingly steep sloping sides), turrets, dormers, and iron cresting. Barnaby built the home at the height of his business success. He opened J. B. Barnaby & Co., which grew to become a large and trendy clothing store, in 1869 and dabbled in politics, holding a seat on the city council for nine years but narrowly losing a bid for governor as well as one for the U.S. House of Representatives. The Barnaby name isn't without scandal in Rhode Island. In 1891—two years after his death—Barnaby's widow, Josephine, died from arsenic poison after drinking laced whiskey. Family physician Dr. Thomas Thatcher Graves was convicted of the murder but committed suicide while awaiting trial after an appeal overturned his verdict. In

---

Due to ongoing restorations, tours are not recommended for children under 16.

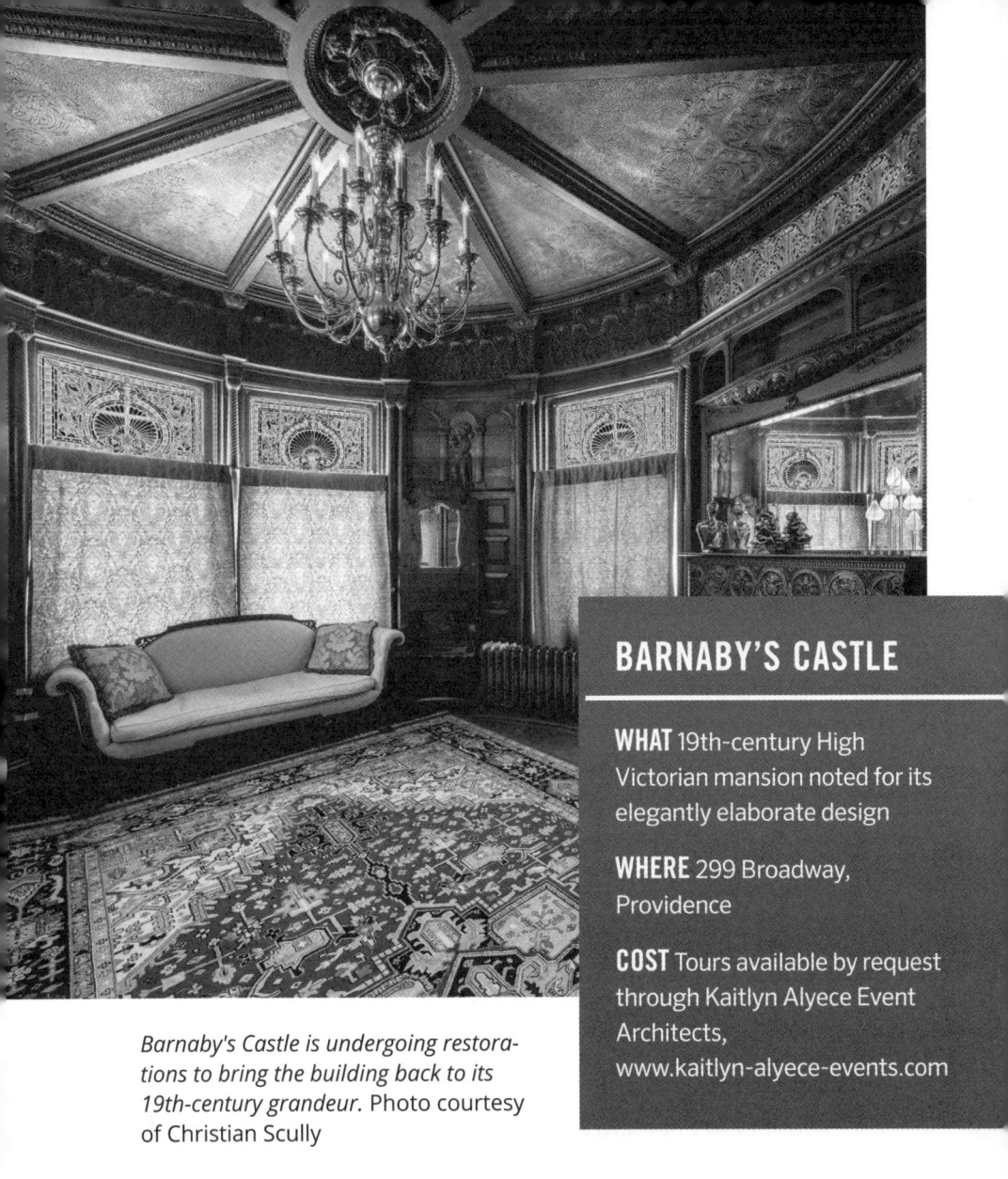

Barnaby's Castle is undergoing restorations to bring the building back to its 19th-century grandeur. Photo courtesy of Christian Scully

BARNABY'S CASTLE

WHAT 19th-century High Victorian mansion noted for its elegantly elaborate design

WHERE 299 Broadway, Providence

COST Tours available by request through Kaitlyn Alyece Event Architects, www.kaitlyn-alyece-events.com

recent years, the mansion has gained popularity as an event space, with fees going toward house restorations. This provides an opportunity for the curious to experience the castle in majestic revelry befitting its history and for the local community to help build pride of place as they contribute to its return to grandeur.

19 ROSE ISLAND LIGHTHOUSE

Where can you vacation in a lighthouse?

It's hard—if not impossible—not to be amazed by the beauty of the Rose Island Lighthouse or the once-in-a-lifetime vacation available there. Rose Island once housed fortifications built to defend Newport during the American Revolution. In 1870, the Rose Island Lighthouse was built in Newport to accommodate shipping traffic in the East Passage of Narragansett Bay. It served as a functioning lighthouse until 1970, when the newly built Newport Bridge made it obsolete as a navigational aid. In 1984, the Rose Island Lighthouse Foundation was formed to preserve, maintain, and operate the lighthouse, which was listed on the National Register of Historic Places in 1987. Today, the lighthouse, named for its island home, is a vacation destination like no other available in Rhode Island. Reachable only by the foundation's lobster boat (named *Starfish*), guests are treated to a stay of romanticism, tranquility, and beauty and encouraged to unplug. There is limited electricity but no Wi-Fi on the island. An overnight stay here is best accompanied by picnics—there's no evening transportation off the island for dinner—fishing, taking pictures, and a leisurely walk around the lighthouse or the island, unless you're staying during bird nesting season from March 1 to August 15, when access is limited. Guests are also welcome to explore the lighthouse museum and the Fort Hamilton Barracks, which were constructed here from 1798 to 1801. Modern amenities may be limited, but they're hardly missed while relishing awe-inspiring views and the simple pleasure of getting away from it all.

The lighthouse, on Rose Island in Narragansett Bay, is preserved and operated by the Rose Island Lighthouse Foundation. Photo courtesy of Kate Grasso Photography

ROSE ISLAND LIGHTHOUSE

WHAT A lighthouse bed and breakfast

WHERE Rose Island, Newport

COST Rooms start at $125 per night (2017 rates)

If you plan to fish, make sure you stock a cooler with ice; no refrigeration is available in the lighthouse.

39

20 DRAGON RACES

Where can you see authentic Chinese dragon boat races in Rhode Island?

Still the only of its kind in the United States—because participants use fiberglass Taiwanese-style dragon boats from Taiwan and participate in flag-catching—the Rhode Island Chinese Dragon Boat Races & Taiwan Day Festival continues to be one of the state's most wonderfully embraced annual festivals. Held annually in September since 1999 by the Blackstone Valley Tourism Council and the City of Pawtucket, the races and festival are modeled after the Chinese tradition that began more than 2,000 years ago as a tribute to the Chinese water deity, the dragon, to ask for rain needed for a plentiful harvest. Said to be the most respected of the Chinese zodiac figures, the dragon is a revered symbol of water and prosperity. Stories also point to a tribute to beloved poet Qu Yuan, whom villagers tried to save by racing into the river after he leaped to his death during a time of great political turmoil. The races are said to be a reenactment of this act of love and sorrow. Blackstone Valley's race is sanctioned by the Eastern Boat Association and offers two divisions, so both club teams and amateurs can get in on the fun. The festival includes cultural performances, Taiwanese arts and crafts vendors, interactive tables, a popular Chinese dumpling eating contest, and dancers.

This is a great family-friendly event, so bring the children for an afternoon of learning and play.

The dragon boat races are part of the annual Taiwan Day Festival. Photo courtesy of James Toomey, Blackstone Valley Tourism Council

CHINESE DRAGON BOAT RACES

WHAT Yearly boat race held during the Taiwan Day Festival to celebrate Chinese culture and heritage

WHERE Festival Pier, 50 Tim Healey Way, Pawtucket

COST Race registration at www.dragonboatri.com

21 MUSÉE PATAMÉCANIQUE

Calling it a "cabinet of curiosities" is about as far as Musée Patamécanique founder Neil Salley is likely to go into revealing just what he has behind the curtains of his mysterious museum—and that includes its location. So obscure is this collection of patamechanics—a term Salley himself coined while a graduate student at the Rhode Island School of Design to describe objects that are "evidence of a realm or entity that exists supplementary to this one"—that most accounts of it report it's only accessible to those seen fit to enter. Tours, available upon request through the museum's website, when they are given at all, begin in downtown Bristol at sunset—yes, they are conducted only in the evening. They include a narrated walk to the Musée's secret location and are immersive and interactive, giving visitors an overview of pataphysics, which is best summed up, it seems, as a branch of philosophy centered on fantastic phenomena, and through various exhibits and installations that one critic called "an intellectual hall of mirrors." To divulge more about what's inside the hallowed halls of this one-of-a-kind place would be a disservice to its origins and ideals as well as to the idea of playful fun and sport.

This tour is not recommended for children under 12 both because it is conducted in the dark and because while none of the collection is overtly adult oriented, it's not G-rated either.

Rhode Islander Neil Salley's Musée Patamécanique is kept so secret, visitors aren't given its location until they arrive, meeting for tours at a public spot in Bristol, Rhode Island. Photo courtesy of Neil Salley

MUSÉE PATAMÉCANIQUE

WHAT Private museum dedicated to the pataphysics, a philosophy that embraces the idea of a reality alternative to our own

WHERE It's a secret (until you make a tour appointment), but it's most likely in the historic district of Bristol

COST $20 per person

22 VROOM, VROOM

Where in Rhode Island do cars and history collide?

If you're an enthusiast for both cars and history, this unique museum belongs on your Rhode Island bucket list. Self-described as "more of an art museum than a car museum," the Audrain Automobile Museum opened in 2014 and is home to more than 200 rare vehicles ranging in date from the early 20th century through today, with a special focus on preserving and presenting automobiles relevant to Newport history. Points of interest in this area include Doris Duke's '49 Cadillac Derham limousine and the Vanderbilt family's '41 Cadillac Fleetwood Series 75 Imperial Touring Limo. By displaying between 15 and 20 vehicles at a time in thematic exhibits, the museum provides visitors a walk through time. Recent exhibits included "Drop Dead Tops," "Classic & Fantastic Automobiles from 1945–1965," and "Pre-War Automobiles," featuring vehicles from 1912 to the start of WWII. The Audrain Building itself is a point of interest in Newport. Built from 1902 to 1903 for a wealthy New York merchant who summered in Newport by prominent architect Bruce Price (Emily Post's father), it was important in turn-of-the-century city commerce. It's considered architecturally significant for its two-story, six-shop-front bay makeup.

If you happen to be in town for one of them, theme nights such as Wine & Wheels trivia night are a treat.

The Audrain Automobile Museum in Newport ties classic cars to local history. Photo courtesy of Audrain Car Museum

AUDRAIN AUTOMOBILE MUSEUM

WHAT Museum dedicated to connecting the history of automobiles to the history of American culture

WHERE 222 Bellevue Ave., Newport

COST Adults, $14; seniors, students, and military, $10; children ages 6–17, $8; children ages 5 and under, free

23 VAMPIRE GRAVE

Is there a creature of the night buried in a quiet Rhode Island town?

Vampires are creations of fiction, right? Some people will tell you otherwise, but no matter your stance, it's hard to deny, given an ongoing plethora of entertainment devoted to the subject, a cultural fascination with the vampire. It's said that one of the earliest inspirations for vampire tales came from Rhode Island. Mercy Brown was just 19 years old when she succumbed in 1892 to tuberculosis, which was an extremely deadly and feared disease at that time. She was the third member of her family to die from the disease, and folklore of the day centered on a nonmedical reason for so many family members contracting the same illness: the undead had infected them. As such, when Mercy's brother Edwin grew ill, their father gave permission for his dead relatives to be exhumed. When Mercy's body was discovered to have blood in her heart and liver, she was declared the undead perpetrator. Her heart was extracted and burned, and the ashes were fed to Edwin in hopes of curing him. Unfortunately, Edwin grew sicker still and died about two months later. The likely explanation for Mercy's slow decomposition was that her body had essentially been stored in refrigeration and not yet buried when examined for signs of vampirism. Still, her story has served as inspiration for several creators of vampirism fiction, including a young adult novel and *Almost Mercy*, a major motion picture. Some say she was even the genesis of the character Lucy in Bram Stoker's *Dracula*. Naturally, rumors persist that Mercy continues to haunt her gravesite. Her remains, sans her heart, were eventually buried in the cemetery of the Baptist Church in town.

Was Mercy Brown, who died in 1892 at just 19, really a vampire? More likely an explanation for her body having blood in it months after her death is that her body was so well preserved by refrigeration. Photo courtesy of Josh McGinn; https://www.flickr.com/photos/sven-storm/2926171996

MERCY BROWN GRAVE

WHAT Burial site of a rumored vampire whose story has served as literary and cinematic inspiration

WHERE 467 Ten Rod Rd., Exeter

COST Free

Since Mercy's heart was removed during her exhumation—a noted death sentence for the undead—it's probably safe to say that she won't rise again, and visitors can pay respects with no fear of paying with their lives.

24 AXE THAT

Where can you spend the night in the home of an axe murderer?

Most school-aged children in the area know the story: Lizzie Borden took an axe, gave her mother 40 whacks, and when she saw what she had done, she gave her father 41. Lizzie Borden was 32 years old when she was tried for the axe murders of her father, Andrew Jackson Borden, and stepmother, Abby Durfee Gray, in 1892 at the family's home in Fall River, Massachusetts, about 15 miles outside Providence. Charging Lizzie with the crime was an easy call. Her stories about the events on the day of the double murders were inconsistent. She was said to exhibit strange—almost sociopathic—behaviors in their aftermath, and the family had been at odds with each other since her father's remarriage. At the center of the tension was money. It was widely known that Lizzie feared that her stepmother was after her father's money. Though he lived frugally, Andrew Borden had amassed a small fortune—he was worth about $8 million in today's dollars at the time of his death—and he had begun doling out money through real estate to his new wife's family. Acquitting Lizzie of the crime also wasn't especially hard. Evidence was circumstantial, and police made several errors in the initial stages of their investigation, including not conducting a forensic sweep of her bedroom. After the trial, Lizzie remained in Fall River, but she also remained the crime's prime suspect. The trial was followed by the public in such a way that Lizzie became a celebrity. The fanfare has been compared with modern-day trials, such as that of O. J. Simpson for the murders of his ex-wife and her second husband. Today, the family home

Though Lizzie Borden was acquitted on charges of murdering her father and stepmother with an axe, some still doubt her innocence. Photo courtesy of DkEgy via Wikimedia Commons

LIZZIE BORDEN HOUSE

WHAT Bed-and-breakfast at the home of alleged murderer and local legend Lizzie Borden

WHERE 230 2nd St., Fall River, Massachusetts

COST Rooms start at $220 per night. Tours of the house are adults, $18; seniors & college students, $15; children ages 7–12, $10; children ages 6 and under, free

is a bed-and-breakfast and a popular tourist attraction, and tours are also available. The room where Abby was murdered is reportedly the most popular for spending the night.

The Lizzie Borden "rhyme" is of unknown origin and is inaccurate. Abby Gray suffered 18 or 19 whacks and Andrew Borden a mere 11.

25. BACKSTAGE GALLERY

Where is Providence's most 'signature' art collection?

It's no secret around the city that the Providence Performing Arts Center is a world-class venue for musicals, plays, and the ballet. Agreed to be the unofficial heart of the city's arts and entertainment district, it's a beautiful theater inside and out. Featuring an old-fashioned marquee that lights up the area on performance nights, the theater is pure 1920s opulence inside. Built in 1928, the theater is on the National Register of Historic Places and once was a movie palace. It has been meticulously remodeled and restored to reflect its original elegance. Area theater lovers flock here for Broadway show tours, pre-Broadway runs, and national tour openings. What not everyone knows about is the art gallery of sorts on the walls backstage. PPAC reports visitors are "often surprised and intrigued" by the murals—each drawn by a member of a visiting production and signed by the show's cast and company to commemorate their Providence run. Murals include tributes from the casts of *Avenue Q* (2009), *A Chorus Line* (2009), *A Night With Dame Edna* (2004), and from national tour launches of *Beautiful— The Carole King Musical* (2015), *Beauty and the Beast* (2010), *Evita* (2013), and *Cinderella* (2014).

There's also a mural from The Nutcracker, which plays here every winter holiday season and provides a truly remarkable experience for visitors when the theater is fully decked in Christmas décor.

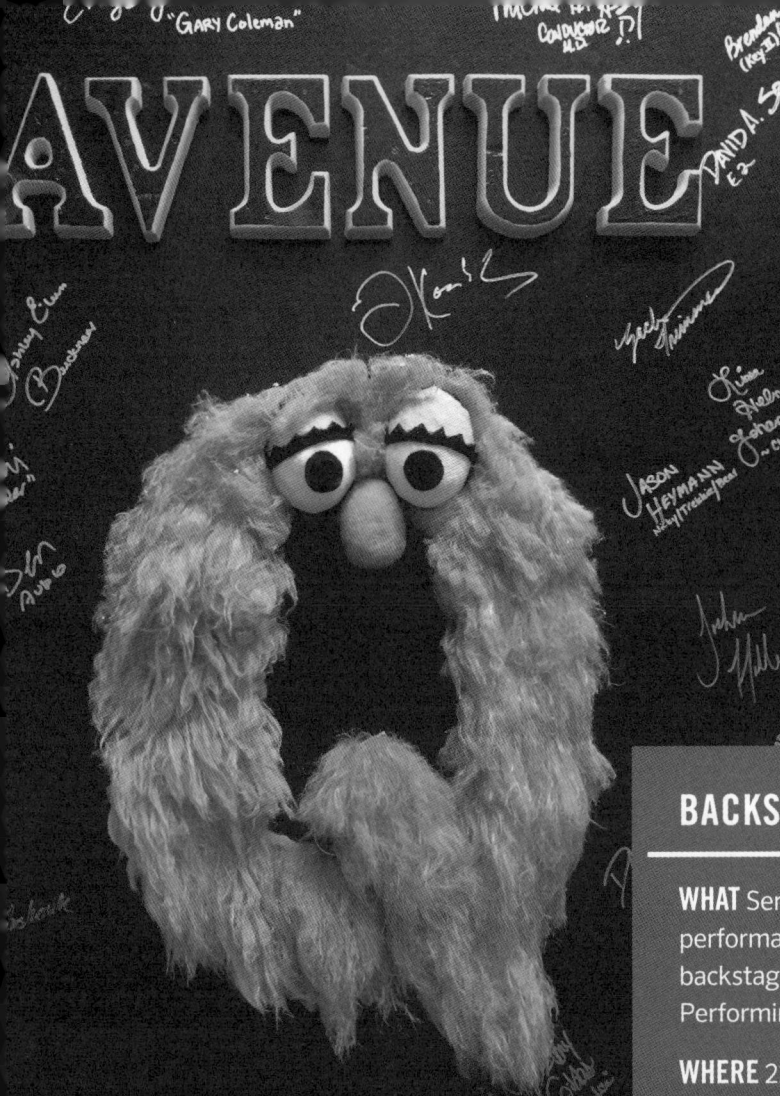

Those lucky enough to get backstage at the Providence Performing Arts Center are treated to its collection of "Show Signatures," posters signed by the casts of visiting productions. Photo courtesy of Providence Performing Arts Center

BACKSTAGE GALLERY

WHAT Series of signed performance murals located backstage at the Providence Performing Arts Center

WHERE 220 Weybosset St., Providence

COST Priceless, if you can get in

26 UNBENEFICIAL PROVENANCE

Did a once common burial practice forever curse one of the city's earliest successful merchants?

When Stephen Harris, a mid-18th-century Providence merchant and American revolutionary, bought his now infamous homestead at 135 Benefit Street (probably in 1785), he likely had no idea the house was already occupied . . . at least underground. Many moons before, around the time the city was first settled, when Benefit Street was narrower and called Back Street, it was customary in Providence for families to bury their dead on their own land. This was because there was no common burial ground until near the start of the American Revolution, when the city's first cemetery was formed. When Back Street was widened (and renamed), most family plots were emptied, but some of the dead, according to various stories, were left behind, including those buried beneath number 135. Legend has it that as soon as Harris took up residence at the house, his good fortune began to turn. The family's finances suffered, and two of his three sons died young and in short succession. Mrs. Harris was reported to have gone mad while living there and could be heard calling out from her room—but in French, the native language of those buried occupants. H. P. Lovecraft believed these stories so strongly that they inspired his story "The Shunned House," a haunted-house tale in which he wrote, "Nor was any child to be born alive in that house for a century and a half," amplifying the rumor that Harris and his second wife, Abigail Cushing, were plagued by a series of stillbirths and early

It is alleged that the house of American revolutionary Stephen Harris was haunted by those buried underneath before a common burial ground was built in the city.

STEPHEN HARRIS HOUSE

WHAT Allegedly haunted house of American revolutionary Stephen Harris and the subject of an H. P. Lovecraft horror story

WHERE 135 Benefit St., Providence

COST None

deaths for their children. Historical research indicates that much of the lore was in fact created by Lovecraft. Abigail's first child did die young, but her other five children lived long lives.

Benefit Street is known as Providence's "mile of history" due to the considerable number of Colonial-era homes lining this cobblestone street that was created "for the benefit of all."

27 FACTORY OF FANTASTIC FINDS

Where's the one must-see shopping center in the state?

When visitors to the state ask Rhode Islanders what shopping experience they must take in during their time here, the answer almost unanimously will be the Fantastic Umbrella Factory. Tucked away in the South County town of Charlestown, it was opened in 1968 on a farmstead, with just one gift shop, but the property's distinctive landscaping turned out to be as much of a draw to some as the shopping. Several perennial gardens adorn the factory and provide an atmosphere that allows visitors to feel they are shopping in someone's backyard. More retailers came in over the years, and today the factory is home to vendors selling handcrafted housewares, clothing, jewelry, and musical instruments, among other items. In 2010, the Small Axe Cafe started satisfying the appetites of hungry customers with local and organic dishes and a BYOB policy. A new General Store specializes in unique gifts and toys, and Axiom, the newest shop, offers vintage eye glasses. David Turano, who has been selling pottery at the complex at Small Axe Productions (with two other crafters) since 1974, and his wife, Linda, purchased the property in 2011 from the original owner. The couple state that their intention for the locale is for it to be "an enjoyable and affordable destination for locals and visitors alike."

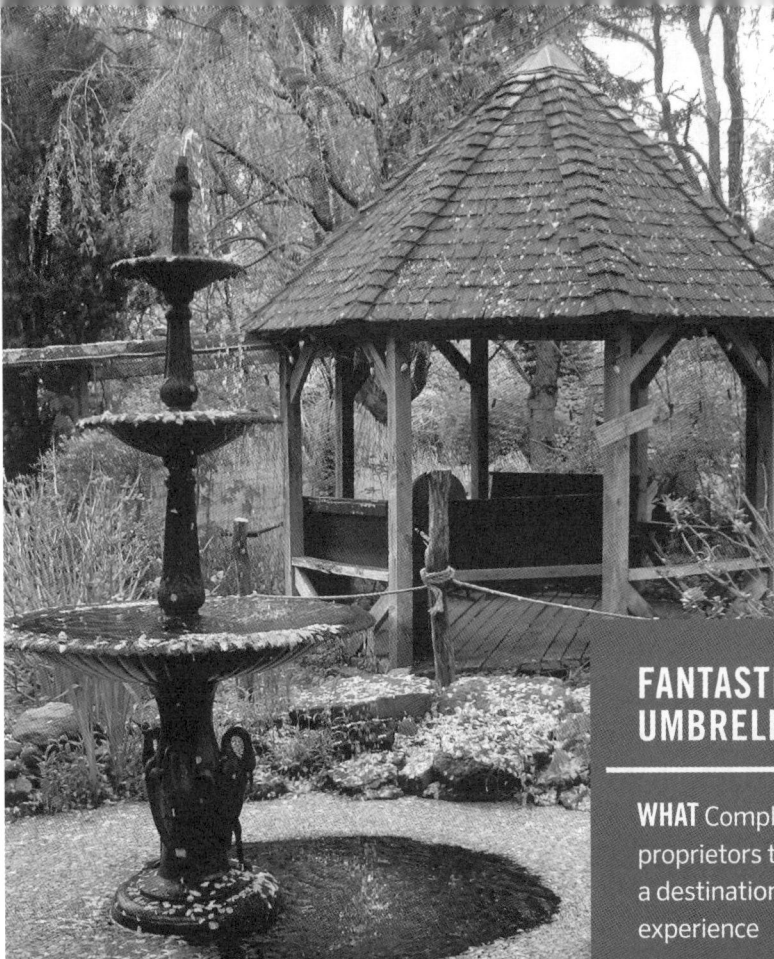

Much more than an ordinary shopping destination, the Fantastic Umbrella Factory is a feast for the eyes. Photo courtesy of the Fantastic Umbrella Factory

FANTASTIC UMBRELLA FACTORY

WHAT Complex of unique proprietors that provides a destination shopping experience

WHERE 4820 Old Post Rd., Charlestown

COST Depends on the store

> The property is home to two goats, three emus, chickens, and ducks. Petting the animals is allowed; feeding them people food is not.

28 IRISH LOT

What's the story behind the mysterious holes in this graveyard's markers?

Tucked in a 30- by 40-foot corner of a historical cemetery in Middletown, Rhode Island, is a cluster of gravesites known as the Irish Lot. Besides housing what are known to be early-19th-century graves of prominent Rhode Islanders, the graveyard has one remarkably distinctive feature. The grave markers have mysterious holes—and no one knows what they are or how they got there. Though experts, including one in graveyard studies, have examined them, only one real theory has emerged—that the headstones are riddled with bullet holes. Evidence for the theory points to the fact that the headstones are slate, which would allow for bullets to have caused the irregular shape of the holes. One non-mysterious element of the lot is how it got its name. Col. George Irish was a lifelong Middletown resident, born there in 1729, who made a name for himself through both his business endeavors and his support of the American Revolution. He owned a West Indies trade ship called *Friendship* as well as farms in Middletown; Hopkintown, Rhode Island; and nearby Stonington, Connecticut. As a grain merchant, he had a strong trade relationship in Virginia, where he conducted business directly with George Washington. As a wealthy landowner, he had the means to loan the Colonial army 3,257 pounds sterling to help fund the burgeoning revolution. He was also a colonel in the First Rhode Island Militia and served in the postwar Newport County Assembly. His grave, showing that he died in October 1801, is the most prominent and easily identifiable burial site in the Irish Lot.

The Irish Lot in Middletown is a small cemetery where some gravestones have mysterious holes that are thought to be from bullets.

IRISH LOT

WHAT Historic cemetery in Middletown, where headstones are rumored to be riddled with bullet holes

WHERE High Street, across from the rear of the Residence Inn and Middletown Post Office

COST None

The cemetery is on the corner of a busy street and is quite compact. Exercise safety precautions when paying your respects.

29 STUCK-UP BRIDGE

Why is there a broken bridge stuck upright in Providence?

Even though its existence could point to a period of less-than-great prosperity in Providence's history, the Crook Point Bascule Bridge has become a local icon of sorts and a favorite photography subject among urban explorers. The bascule bridge—another term for drawbridge—was built in 1908 to service railway travel from the city's old Union Station along the New York, New Haven and Hartford line and was designed by the Scherzer Rolling Lift Bridge Company from Chicago. Measuring 850 feet across, it rose to a 64-degree angle to open a 125-foot-wide water passageway. As railway traffic declined through the 1970s, both Union Station—which now houses nonprofits and a popular restaurant—and the bridge became economic liabilities. Though rail service continued—it was moved to a smaller station in the mid-1980s—the Crook Point bridge faced the chopping block. Demolition costs were such a hardship, though, that the city ultimately decided to leave it intact, fixed in an upright position to allow water vessel passage along the river. Since its abandonment in 1976, the bridge has become a target of both vandalism and fascination among locals and visitors. Though it has severely decayed over the decades, many artists and students have made it the subject of photographs, documentaries, and studies. While many have ventured onto the bridge for such projects or to satisfy their own curiosity, it is considered extremely dangerous to do so. Photographing the bridge can most safely be done at its western entrance—no climbing necessary.

CROOK POINT BASCULE BRIDGE

WHAT An abandoned drawbridge on the Seekonk River

WHERE Western entrance near the intersection of Gano and Williams Sts.

COST None

The Crook Point Bascule Bridge on the Seekonk River has been stuck in its upright position since the 1970s, abandoned because demolition was too costly and declining railway traffic had rendered it unnecessary. Photo courtesy of rprata via Wikimedia Commons

Be sure to also stop by Union Station on Exchange Street to complete your railroad-themed tour.

59

30 HIGHPOINTING FIX

Where is Rhode Island's highest point?

Jerimoth Hill, about 15 miles west of Providence on Route 101 in Foster, might not actually be all that high compared with some hiking spots—it stands at 812 feet, or 247 meters—but it is nonetheless a destination of interest for many, including those interested in the somewhat obscure hobby of highpointing, enthusiasts of which are called highpointers. This activity involves ascending to the highest elevation in any given area. Highpointers create a bucket list-type of goal—hitting the highest point in, for example, each county of a state, each U.S. state, or each continent (the "Seven Summits"). Highpointers and others interested in seeing Rhode Island from its highest point have only been able to do so since around 2005. Before that time, Jerimoth Hill—where the actual summit is a large rock located about one-third of a mile from the road and is accessible by an easy trail—was located on private property, and the property owner prohibited entry. The state of Rhode Island now owns the land and the summit, which previously was owned and used as an observatory by Brown University. As for climbing, Jerimoth Hill doesn't provide much of a physical challenge, but it certainly is a trip worth taking.

The summit area is quite pretty and picture-worthy; bring a camera to record some nice memories.

JERIMOTH HILL

WHAT Rhode Island's highest point

WHERE Route 101, about half a mile from the Connecticut state line and 15 miles west of Providence

COST None

Highpointers, those who seek to climb to the highest spot in a city, state, county, or country, can get their fix at Jerimoth Hill. Photo courtesy of Fredlyfish4 via Wikimedia Commons (1); Photo courtesy of Basheer Tome, reprinted with permission (2): https://www.flickr.com/photos/basheer-tome/10293926046

61

31 SPRING LAKE ARCADE

Where can you visit the world's oldest penny arcade?

The Spring Lake Arcade is one of those places that, regardless of how many testaments to its wonder you hear beforehand, is still amazing to see in person. Nestled in the state's northwest corner, in the Glendale village of Burriville, the arcade proudly carries the title of the world's oldest operating penny arcade business, although it now has game machines that cost more than that to play. The fun began in 1930 when a man named Edmund Reed installed a carnival game called "Walking Charley" next to a pool hall beach business offshore of Spring Lake, a popular summertime recreation spot. The game was followed by penny-operated machines, which quickly became more popular than Walking Charley, and so Reed expanded the penny games. He eventually took over the pool hall and passed it down to his son-in-law, who in turn operated it until today's proprietor—and coin-operated machine collector—John Bateman took it over in the late 1980s. Since then the arcade has seen some modernization, adding more fashionable machines to satisfy changing desires among the patrons who flock here every June through Labor Day. The biggest draw, however, continues to be the penny machines and antique games, some of them dating to the 1920s.

Spring Lake Arcade is the country's oldest penny arcade. Photo courtesy of John Bateman, Spring Lake Arcade

SPRING LAKE ARCADE

WHAT World's oldest arcade with penny machines

WHERE 52 Old Hillside Dr., Glendale

COST Games start at $0.01 a turn

Admittance to the arcade itself is free, but there is a nominal fee for Spring Lake, which can change each summer. Be sure to check with the town of Burriville, Rhode Island, for up-to-date prices.

63

32 PRESIDENTIAL PORTRAIT

Where can you view one of the most famous portraits in U.S. history?

The nation's first president, George Washington, was reportedly a little shy about having his likeness captured. While we can all be thankful that he relented later in life—imagine not having any idea what Mr. Washington looked like—Rhode Islanders are extra thankful that one of his favorite portraitists was one of their own. Gilbert Stuart (1755-1828) is unarguably one of the state's most famous natives and one of the country's leading masters of his craft. Historical accounts relate that Gilbert showed exceptional artistic ability by the age of six and lived abroad during his teenage and early adult years to develop his talent, but it wasn't until moving to Philadelphia in the early to mid-1790s that he truly blossomed. He went on to become the portraitist of choice in prestigious circles and by the end of his career had painted portraits of six U.S. presidents, but his most esteemed subject was George Washington. Gilbert painted a series of portraits of the president—and amassed a small fortune selling reproductions—with the most famous being *The Athenaeum*, an unfinished painting that appears on the one-dollar bill and is owned by the National Portrait Gallery in Washington, DC, and the Museum of Fine Arts in Boston. Another Gilbert portrait of Washington, a copy of which hangs in the East Room of the White House, is the Lansdowne portrait, which depicts the president renouncing a third term. At the Rhode Island State House, an original portrait commissioned by the state legislature following Washington's death in 1799 hangs over the fireplace.

GILBERT STUART PORTRAIT

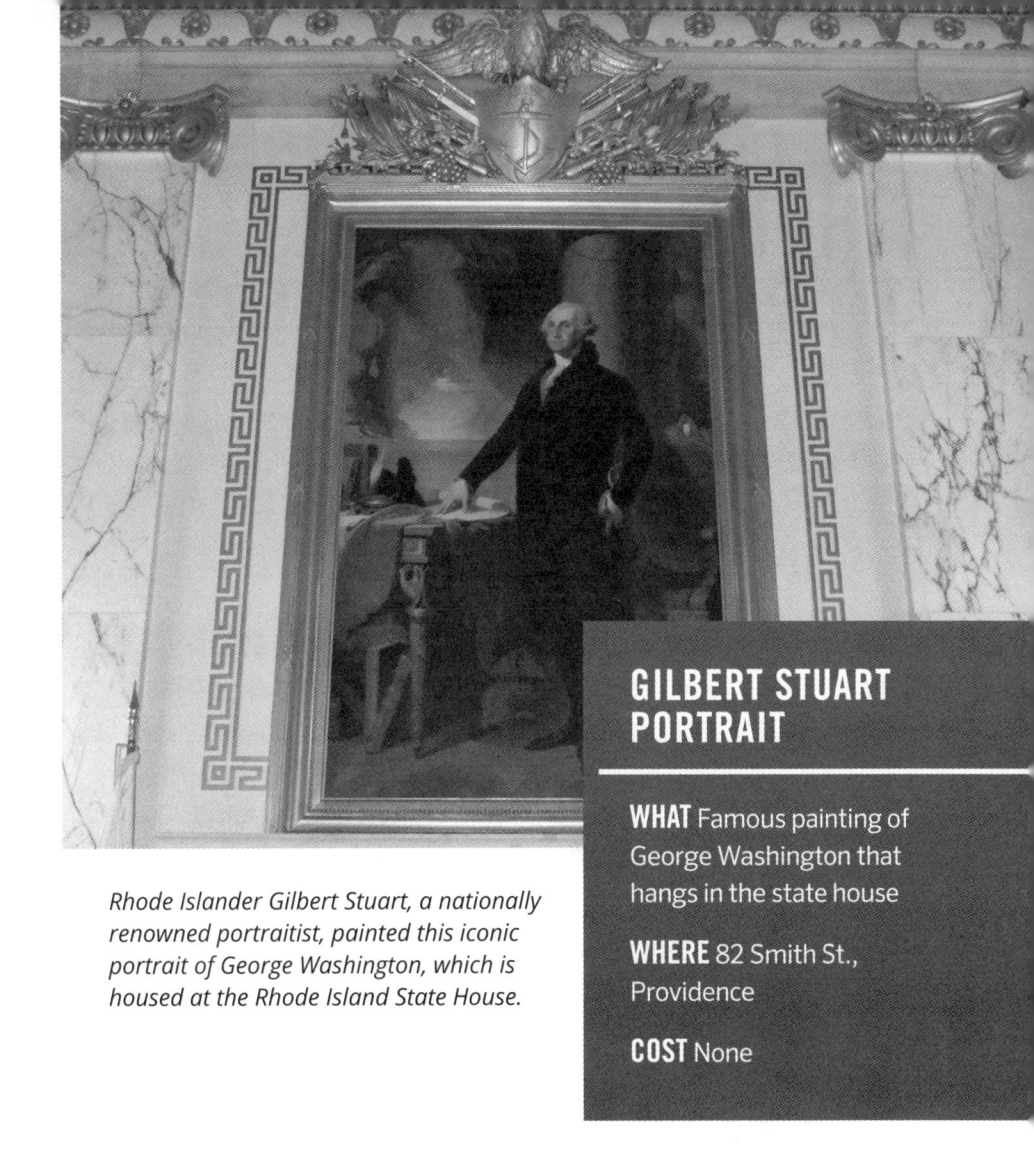

WHAT Famous painting of George Washington that hangs in the state house

WHERE 82 Smith St., Providence

COST None

Rhode Islander Gilbert Stuart, a nationally renowned portraitist, painted this iconic portrait of George Washington, which is housed at the Rhode Island State House.

Gilbert was buried in Boston but without a marker because the family could not afford one, and the exact location of his grave is unknown. There is a monument for his family at the Common Burying Ground in Newport, where Gilbert lived for a short time during his childhood.

33. WE'LL DRINK TO THAT—RHODE ISLAND'S REFUSAL TO RATIFY PROHIBITION

Where can you toast Providence's rebellious ways at a still-operating speakeasy?

Rhode Islanders weren't the only folks to object to Prohibition, the constitutional outlawing of the production, transportation, and sale of alcohol across the country from 1920 to 1933. And though the dry period wasn't exactly observed nationwide—one of the reasons it was eventually repealed was ineffectual enforcement—Rhode Island was the only state that refused to ratify the 18th Amendment to the U.S. Constitution that made it law. Rhode Island, founded in a spirit of welcoming the rebellious and those wanting freedom from overbearing religious intolerance, had a large Irish-Catholic and immigrant population that largely rejected the temperance movement as puritanical persecution. (Indeed, many Prohibition supporters blamed the rise of crime and drunkards on late-19th- and early-20th-century immigration.) Still, enough states did ratify the measure to make it official, and while it wasn't illegal to consume alcoholic drinks, it was illegal to buy and sell them. Out of necessity comes invention, though, and thus was born the speakeasy—an illegal saloon named for the need to speak quietly about such an establishment—and they were everywhere, Rhode Island included. Several well-known speakeasies were in Providence—the local police force famously hung out with their whiskies at what is now the Biltmore hotel downtown—and Camille's, a still-standing favorite on Federal Hill, was among the most popular. Patrons here imbibed booze made in the restaurant's cellar,

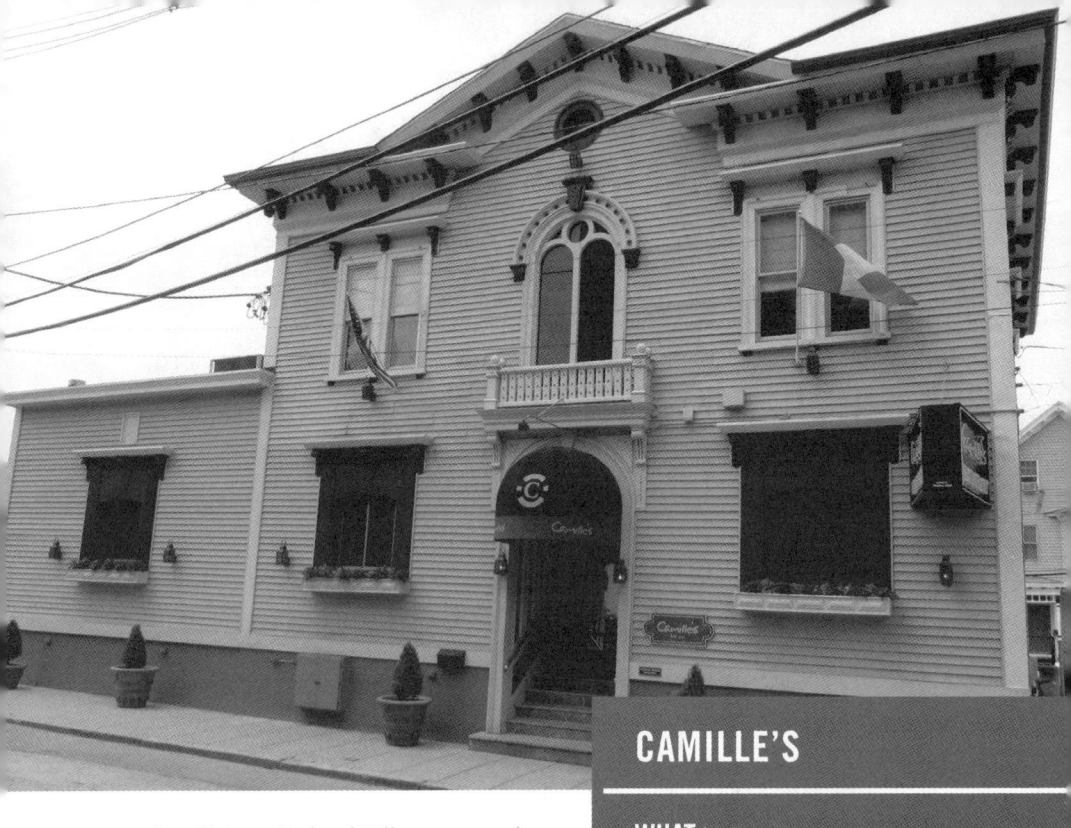

Camille's on Federal Hill was a speakeasy during Prohibition, which Rhode Island never adopted as law. Photo courtesy of Leonard J. DeFrancisci via Wikimedia Commons

CAMILLE'S

WHAT Italian restaurant on Federal Hill that operated as a speakeasy during Prohibition

WHERE 71 Bradford St.

COST Depends on your favorite libation

consuming it from coffee cups and behind curtains hung around private alcoves in the dining room. Patrons today won't have to go through such measures to enjoy a cocktail at Camille's, but a visit here is still just as pleasurable.

Today's "speakeasies" are themed bars, offering a throwback vibe to the era. A couple of good ones in Providence are Justine's (9 Olneyville Square) and The Avery (18 Luongo Square).

34 FLYING HORSE CAROUSEL

Where can you ride the country's oldest operating carousel with horses suspended from chains?

Long before country/pop icon Taylor Swift set up camp here, Watch Hill held a well-earned reputation as the hottest spot for summer in Rhode Island. Though the fact that it houses the Flying Horse Carousel isn't its principal draw—that title likely belongs to the area's majestic beaches, stunning views, and scrumptious dining—it certainly adds to Watch Hill's charm, not to mention its historical significance. Built around 1876 by the Charles W. Dare Company, it is the oldest operating carousel in which horses are suspended by chains in the United States. Don't confuse this carousel with the equally historic Flying Horses Carousel in Oak Bluffs, Massachusetts, which is the country's oldest operating platform carousel. The carousel first belonged to a traveling carnival until it was abandoned in Watch Hill in 1879. Until 1914, when it was electrified, it was operated by a hand-cranked organ. It has undergone renovations and restorations from time to time, losing some elements to wear and tear and the weather—three chariots were lost to the New England Hurricane of 1938—all the while maintaining its appeal to the young and young at heart.

If carousels and historical landmarks are among your passions, you'll also want to visit the Crescent Park Looff Carousel in East Providence, which is also a designated National Historic Landmark.

Watch Hill's Flying Horse Carousel is a popular spot for summer fun and the country's oldest carousel with horses suspended on chains. Photo courtesy of Robellin via Wikimedia Commons

FLYING HORSE CAROUSEL

WHAT The oldest operating carousel with horses suspended from chains in the United States

WHERE 151 Bay St., Westerly

COST Under $2

It was listed on the National Register of Historic Places in 1980 and named a National Historic Landmark in 1987. Open annually from June until Labor Day, the carousel can accommodate 20 riders at a time and allows younger children to enjoy this childhood tradition.

35 INDUSTRIAL INVENTION

Where is the birthplace of the American Industrial Revolution?

Blackstone Valley, Rhode Island, just outside of Providence, is filled with historical sites that pay tribute to its place in developing Rhode Island and the country. An area jewel is the Slater Mill Historic Site, which includes the restored buildings of the Slater Mill—dubbed the birthplace of the American Industrial Revolution. Samuel Slater (1768–1835) immigrated to the still young United States at the tender age of 21 after apprenticing as a textile machinist in the United Kingdom, bringing the skill with him and setting up shop in Pawtucket, Rhode Island. He later would be known in his homeland as "Slater the Traitor" for this perceived treachery, but here he is celebrated as one of the early shapers of the state's economy. Slater Mill was the first successful cotton-spinning factory in the United States, operating this way until 1829 but utilized as a manufacturing center until 1921. When it closed, local businessmen organized to purchase and restore the mill, which soon began operating as a museum. Slater Mill was designated a National Historic Landmark in 1966. Additional structures of importance—including the Sylvanus Brown House, an 18th-century artisan cottage that was home to one of Slater's first pattern makers—were later located here, and

---

The museum is open only by appointment from December through February but generously opens its doors seven days per week from July 4th through Labor Day.

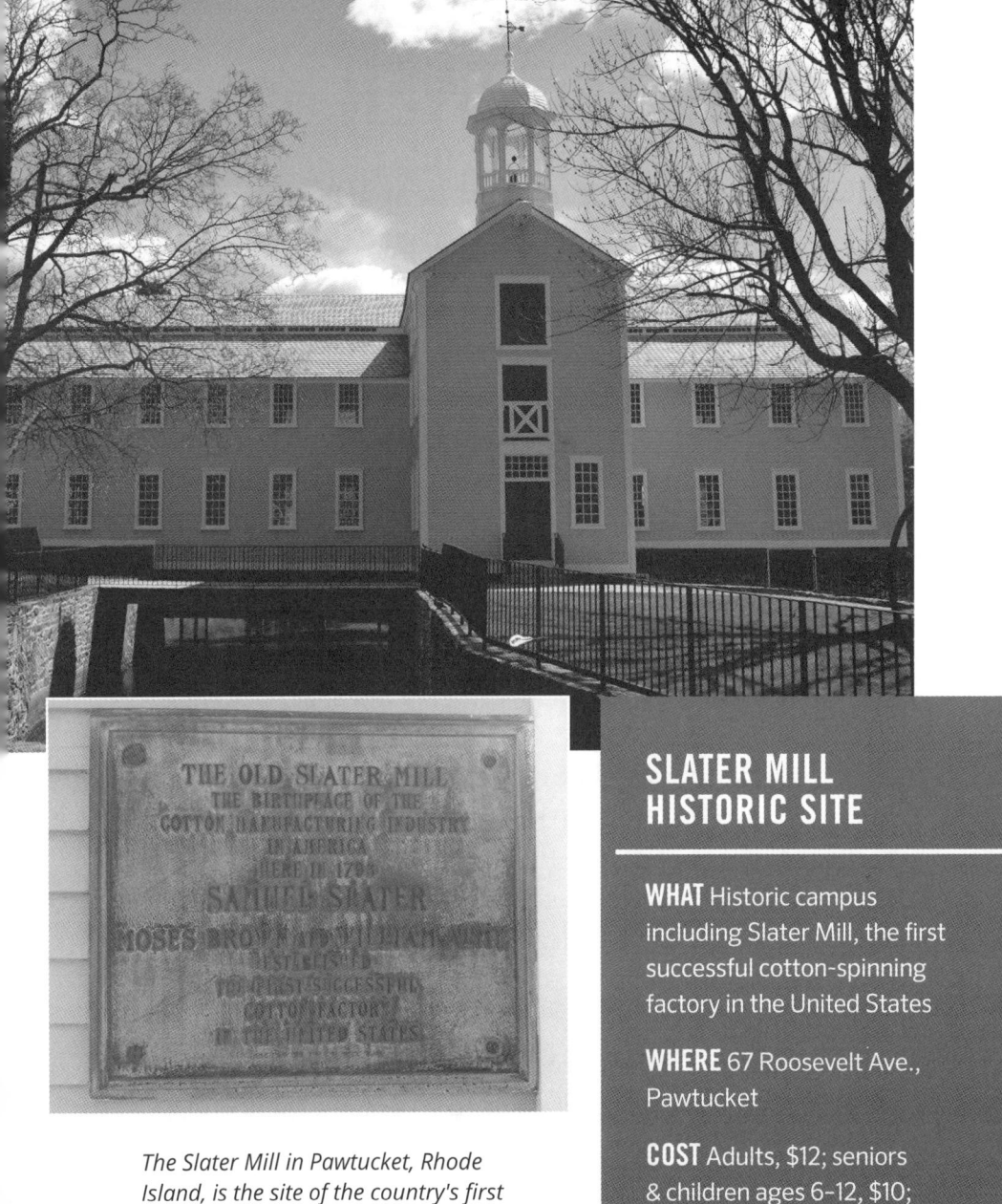

The Slater Mill in Pawtucket, Rhode Island, is the site of the country's first cotton mill, which started the American Industrial Revolution. Photo courtesy of James Toomey for Blackstone Valley Tourism Council (1) Photo courtesy of author (2)

SLATER MILL HISTORIC SITE

WHAT Historic campus including Slater Mill, the first successful cotton-spinning factory in the United States

WHERE 67 Roosevelt Ave., Pawtucket

COST Adults, $12; seniors & children ages 6–12, $10; children ages 5 and under, free

the site was named the Slater Mill Historic Site. Today, visitors can take in three historic buildings, a gift shop, an exhibition space, and the Hodgson Rotary Park.

36 COGSWELL TOWER

Is this landmark the state's best-kept historical secret?

Though the views from inside are breathtaking and the story behind it is an important part of Rhode Island's history, Cogswell Tower inside Jenks Park in Central Falls remains one of the state's best-kept secrets despite being a landmark that is more than 100 years old. The tower was built in 1904 as a gift to the city from Caroline Cogswell, a wealthy widow and philanthropist, and at 70 feet tall, stands as Central Falls' highest point. It stands on top of Dexter's Ledge, home to an important piece of history. During King Philip's War (1675–1678), fought between Indian tribes and English colonists (and their native allies), Dexter's Ledge served as a scouting point for Native Americans. They were watching for Plymouth colonist Capt. Michael Pierce and, able to see him coming, were able to ambush the English troops during what became known as "Pierce's Fight"; that battle took place at nearby Pierce Park. Since its erection, Cogswell Tower has been a centerpiece in Central Falls' story and appears on the city seal. Until very recently visitors could only access the tower during special events, making it not so accessible to the average visitor. That seems to be easing, with tours being scheduled, but those remain limited. Jenks Park was built in 1890 on donated land and was listed on the National Register of Historic Places in 1979.

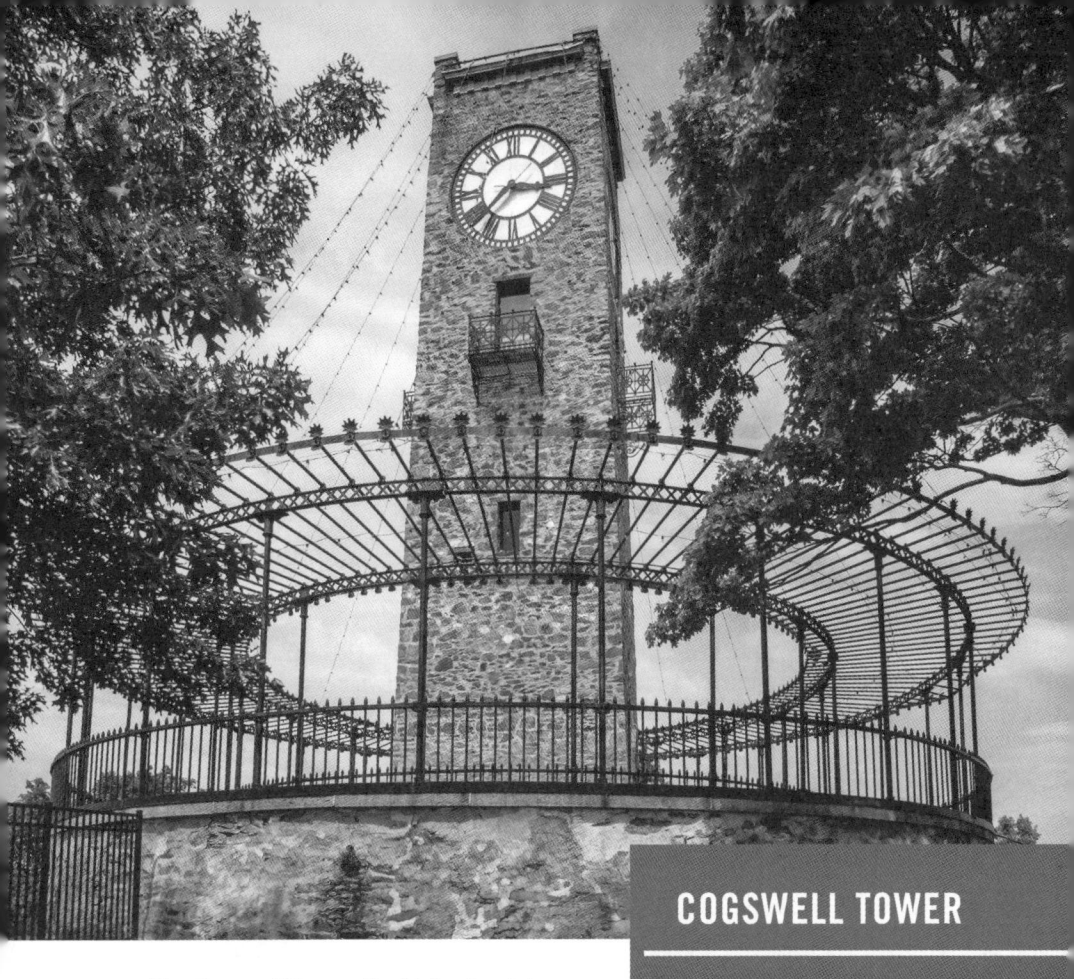

The Cogswell Tower, the highest point in Central Falls, stands atop Dexter's Ledge, which was used as a lookout spot during King Philip's War. Photo courtesy of Kenneth C. Zirkel via Wikimedia Commons

COGSWELL TOWER

WHAT Landmark that offers 360-degree views reaching to the Providence skyline

WHERE 580 Broad St., Central Falls

COST None

If you do visit, be prepared to climb— you'll be going up 70 feet worth of stairs.

73

37 SEABEE MUSEUM

Where can you learn about this unique branch of the U.S. Navy from its original home?

What exactly is a Seabee? Unless you're a member of the military or a scholar (professional or amateur) of its history, you might not know. But a visit to the Seabee Museum & Memorial Park in North Kingstown will change all that and leave you fascinated by this little-known piece of Rhode Island history. Seabees—U.S. Navy Construction Battalions—started serving their country at the onset of World War II to replace a civilian contingent that had been building infrastructure overseas, with the first battalions established at a then-new naval base in Davisville, Rhode Island. Seabees—so named for the initials "C. B."—continued to serve during war times through the Korean War, Vietnam War, and in today's war on terrorism, but the Davisville base was closed in 1994. Thankfully, a group of volunteers—the museum states it was built by and is run by Seabees—now operates a museum and memorial park to keep the contingent's legacy alive. Those not familiar with the museum may first notice the Seabee statue, a monument to the battalions' logo. In 1942, a Navy lieutenant asked a Rhode Island native, a civilian known for his artistic

---

The museum changes its hours seasonally. Visitors can see the museum on Wednesday, Friday, and Saturday during summer hours (May-November) and on Wednesdays and Saturdays during the rest of the year.

The Seabee Museum in North Kingstown honors a division of the U.S. Navy begun here. Photo courtesy of kimvette via Wikimedia Commons

SEABEE MUSEUM & MEMORIAL PARK

WHAT Museum dedicated to the U.S. Navy Construction Battalions, aka Seabees

WHERE 21 Iafrate Way, North Kingstown

COST Admittance is free of charge; donations are accepted

talent, to design a mascot, pictured here. The design incorporated the bee for its reputation as a busy worker that will sting when provoked—much like the Seabee servant whose motto is "We build, we fight."

38 BIG NAZO PUPPETS

Why are monsters sometimes roaming downtown streets?

The first time someone sees them, the reaction is quick and fierce—what exactly are those life-sized monsters doing in downtown Providence? The Big Nazo puppets, as they are affectionately known, belong to Big Nazo, a Providence-based touring performance group of "visual artists, puppet performers, and masked musicians." The group was founded by then-recent Rhode Island School of Design graduate Erminio Pinque, the son of Italian immigrants, after returning from some time as a one-man show performer in Europe, including Italy. It was at this stop that he gained the nickname "Big Nazo"—translating into "big nose." He completed an apprenticeship with a puppeteer and with a partner developed what is now considered a staple of the city's thriving arts scene. The group performs at various events and festivals and in the past has appeared at the Providence Arts Festival and NecronomiCon, a conference dedicated to the darker side of literary arts and famed Providence weird author H. P. Lovecraft. It's more possible you'll run into a puppet in action around the city, as inspiration sometimes drives their master out onto the streets.

Follow the group's website, www.bignazo.com, for updates on performance dates.

BIG NAZO

PO BOX 5742, PROVIDENCE, RI 02903 (401) 831-9652 www.bignazo.com

The Big Nazo puppets are the mascots of a Providence-based performing arts troupe. Photo courtesy of Big Nazo

BIG NAZO PUPPETS

WHAT Props used by performance troop Big Nazo

WHERE Wherever inspiration strikes

COST None

39 JOHNNY CAKES

How did Rhode Islanders come to love this cornmeal pancake?

Rhode Islanders are very fond of their traditions and claims to fame, which goes halfway to explaining their full-on embrace of some seemingly odd foods. The johnny cake, a fried cornmeal concoction commonly placed on the table as a breakfast treat—perhaps in lieu of a pancake—or as dinner bread is eaten up here. It's historically presumed to have originated as a Colonial-era dish, adapted from Native American tribes who grew corn widely here. That's where agreement on the dish ends. Some factions believe it was named after a native tribe—Shawnee—but others say it was taken from "journeycake," an English term used to describe the food's durability during long sea voyages. Some favor a recipe that mixes cornmeal with salt and cold milk that yields a large, crisp cake, and others swear by a recipe that mixes cornmeal with salt and boiling water, which makes a smaller but thicker cake. The days of public feuds on the subject may be over—there was once a cookoff at the State House that ended in a fistfight—but everyone has their favorite way of making and dressing the dish and their favorite place to order it. The owners of Kenyon's Grist Mill, which bills itself as the largest seller of johnny cake mix, favor the latter recipe. The business has been in operation since 1696, although the current building has stood since 1886 and claims to be Rhode Island's oldest manufacturing business. The mill offers tours of its building and facilities during several events held throughout the year.

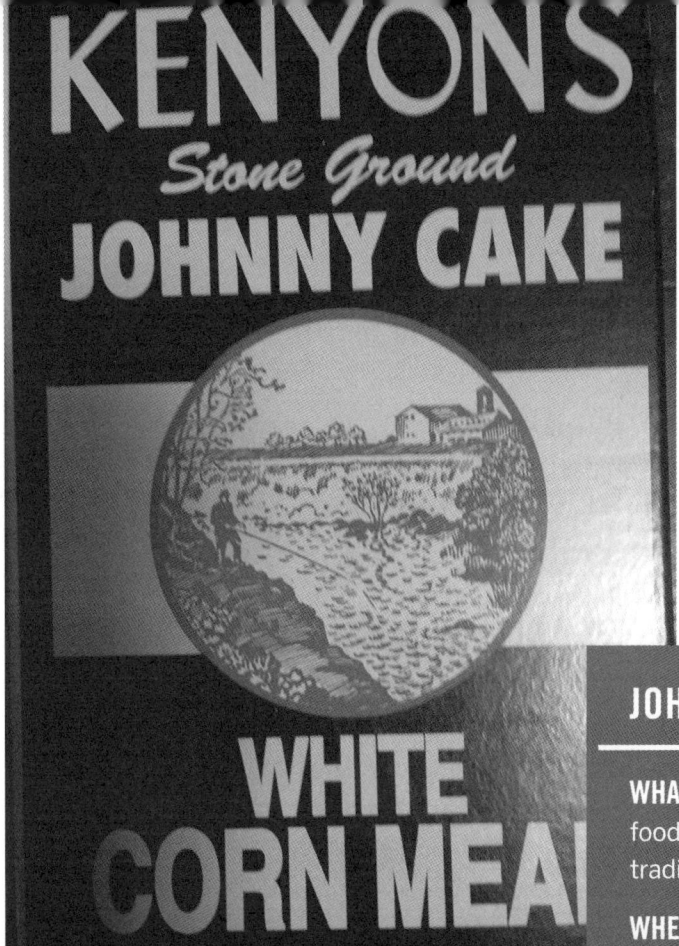

Kenyon's Grist Mill, which bills itself as the largest producer of johnny cake mix, has been in operation since 1696.

JOHNNY CAKES

WHAT Rhode Island breakfast food staple and culinary tradition

WHERE Kenyon's Grist Mill is at 21 Glen Rock Rd., West Kingston. Johnny cakes are served in various restaurants throughout the state

COST Depends on events at the grist mill and a particular restaurant

If you try your hand at cooking the cakes at home, be sure to follow directions carefully. A tasty johnny cake is all in the right mixing.

40 MUSEUM OF WORK AND CULTURE

Where can you take in the history of the "most French city in America"?

Sometimes even in a city and state where history is not only honored but celebrated and esteemed, some of an area's most alluring cultural offerings don't get the attention they deserve. Such is the case with Woonsocket's Museum of Work and Culture, which serves to share the stories of French-Canadian immigrants who came in search of a better life to work in Rhode Island's mills and factories in the late 19th and early 20th centuries. A journey through the museum's six walk-through displays—arranged in chronological order to show the transition from arriving in Woonsocket to building a life here—takes visitors along the immigrants' immersion into a brand-new world and their lasting impact on the town they would come to call home. Exhibits include re-creations of a Quebec farm house, a textile mill shop floor, and a triple-decker home parlor, as well as movies, letters, and photographs. By 1900, about 72 percent of Woonsocket's population was French-Canadian—roughly one-quarter of Quebec residents had come here—earning it a reputation for a time as "the most French city in America." Immigrants carried their culture here, speaking French and forming their communities around the Catholic Church. Today, French-Canadians are the largest ethnic group in Woonsocket, which is home to the American-French Genealogical Society. Fittingly, the museum is housed in an old mill in the city's historic Market Square.

Woonsocket's Museum of Work and Culture pays tribute to the French-Canadian immigrants who helped develop the town in the late 19th and early 20th centuries. Photo courtesy of the Museum of Work and Culture

MUSEUM OF WORK AND CULTURE

WHAT Museum dedicated to immigrants who shaped the lasting French cultures of Woonsocket and other Rhode Island mill towns in the late 19th and early 20th centuries.

WHERE 42 South Main St., Woonsocket

COST Adults, $8; students & seniors, $6; children ages 9 and under, free

Don't forget to visit the museum's gift shop, which offers some excellent reading material for those interested in further study of Rhode Island's French culture.

41 FAVORITE TOYS

Why are there giant Mr. Potato Heads across the state?

Since the toy's creator, Hasbro, is headquartered here and because who doesn't love them, it made sense that Mr. Potato Head was the inspiration behind a civic pride and tourism-attraction campaign executed in 2000. Dozens—about 40—were created for the effort, making six-foot, fiberglass, themed Mr. Potato Heads and placing them in key spots around the state, with the famous Chicago artist-decorated cows in mind. The new travel ambassador wasn't as successful a branding tool as officials had hoped. In fact, the "Tourist Tater" statue was controversial and taken down during the campaign because of complaints that it appeared racist. Painted deep brown and adorned with an ill-fitting Hawaiian shirt, some thought it made the statue look like it was poking fun at some racial stereotypes. Still, Rhode Islanders and visitors remain enthralled by the statues, about eight of which remain on display. These include the Mr. Potato Head at Hasbro Headquarters in Pawtucket, "Regular Joe Potato" at a Dunkin' Donuts in Warren, and "Elephant Potato Head" behind the town hall in Chepachet. Wearing a baseball cap emblazoned with "Betty," this statue is in tribute to Little Bet, an elephant that was gunned down in the town in the 1820s.

The flagship Mr. Potato Head statue outside the company's Pawtucket headquarters presents a prime photo op.

MR. POTATO HEAD STATUES

WHAT Mr. Potato Head statues created in 2000 for a civic pride campaign. Out of the dozens made, only a handful still exist.

WHERE Various locations throughout the state

COST None

The patriotic Mr. Potato Head visits the Bristol 4th of July parade but doesn't come out at any other time during the year, so be sure to catch him then if you want a peek.

42 DOYLE'S HAUNTING GROUND

Is a mayor once laid in state at City Hall haunting its workers?

Ever hear the one about the Providence mayor who after dying in 1886 has actually remained inside its walls—first in his final resting place and then as a ghost? Mayor Thomas Doyle served three terms, the last ending in 1886, and held the record for the city's second-longest-serving mayor for more than 100 years. Rumors have long circulated inside and outside Providence City Hall that Doyle was buried here and hasn't left since. Reports of ghostly instances include hearing unexplainable whispering, smelling cigar smoke when no one was around with one, and hearing footsteps where no one was walking. The popular TV show *Ghost Hunters* even did an episode on the building, but documented investigations have turned up little evidence. This may be because the building isn't haunted, since Doyle was not buried here. He was laid in state at City Hall—he was an extremely popular political figure, and his funeral

---

Providence's city archives, housed in the building, are a treasure trove of artifacts and documents, including the city's original 1647 proclamation and 1648 city charter.

Some say a former, longtime Providence mayor still roams City Hall, many, many years after his death. Photo courtesy of Kenneth C. Zirkel via Wikimedia Commons

SWAN POINT CEMETERY

WHAT Rumored haunting spot of former mayor

WHERE 25 Dorrance St., Providence

COST None

was well attended—but he's buried in Swan Point Cemetery. It's possible, however, that the lack of evidence might be because actual ghosts at the building are upset that they aren't publicly recognized. It is reported that 12 men died during construction of City Hall in the late 1870s, so it just might be their ghosts walking around its storied halls and staircases.

43 FLEUR-DE-LYS STUDIOS

What is Providence's most eccentric example of historic architecture?

Which Providence building is at once a national landmark, a historic art studio, a respected example of the country's Arts and Crafts movement, and a structure of literary significance? The Fleur-de-Lys Studios is all of those, plus an eye-catching attraction in the city's College Hill neighborhood, which is filled with history at almost every corner. Named by the U.S. Library of Congress as "one of the most distinguished examples of a building designed specifically for use as artists' studios," Fleur-de-Lys Studios was designed and built in 1885 by watercolor and oil artist Sydney Richmond Burleigh (1853–1931) and architect Edmund R. Willson (1853–1906), who also helped designed the Providence Public Library around 1900. It's the building's façade—hand-carved with distinctive ornamentation in the shape of the fleur-de-lis, the emblem traditionally used to depict French royalty and which means "flower of the lily" in English, that has given it a reputation as Providence's most eccentric historical building. This is reinforced by famed Providence horror writer H. P. Lovecraft's use of the building as the home of a character in his work "The Call of Cthulhu." Owned today by the Providence Art Club, the building is still used as artist studios, as requested by Burleigh's widow upon her death in 1939. The studio has been lauded as one of architectural significance since its construction, especially in the Arts and Crafts craze that swept the country—and the world—in the late 19th and early 20th centuries.

The Fleur-de-Lys Studios, in the city's College Hill neighborhood, has been lauded as a beautiful example of the Arts and Crafts movement since its construction in 1885. Photo credit: Nicholas Millard for Providence Warwick Convention & Visitors Bureau

FLEUR-DE-LYS STUDIOS

WHAT Providence's most eccentric historical building

WHERE 7 Thomas St., Providence

COST None for exterior viewing and taking pictures. Visit www.providenceartclub.com for artist events

Make this one stop on a walking tour of Providence's East Side neighborhood to maximize your historic architecture experience.

REVERE BELL (page 118)

NECRONOMICON (page 138)

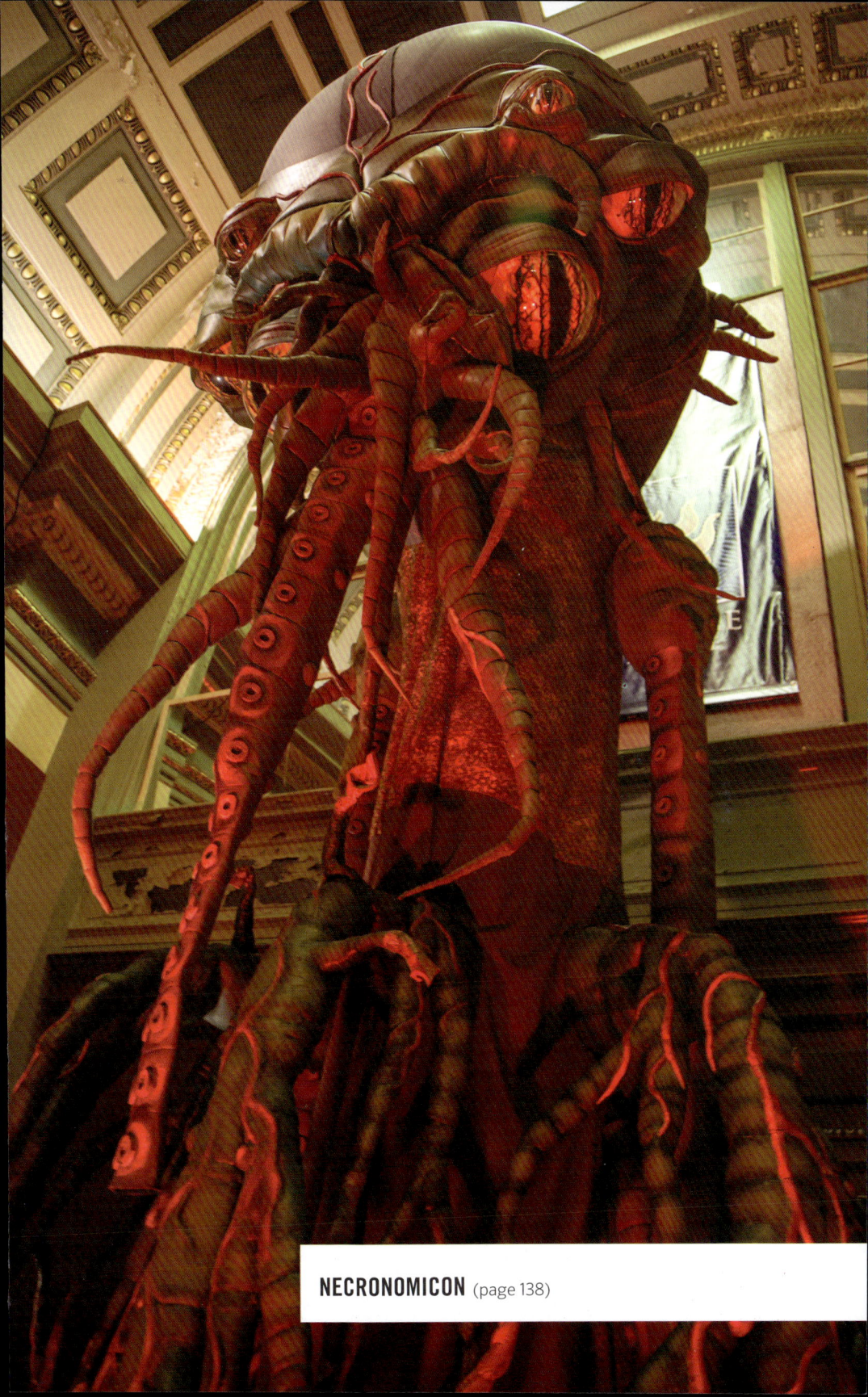

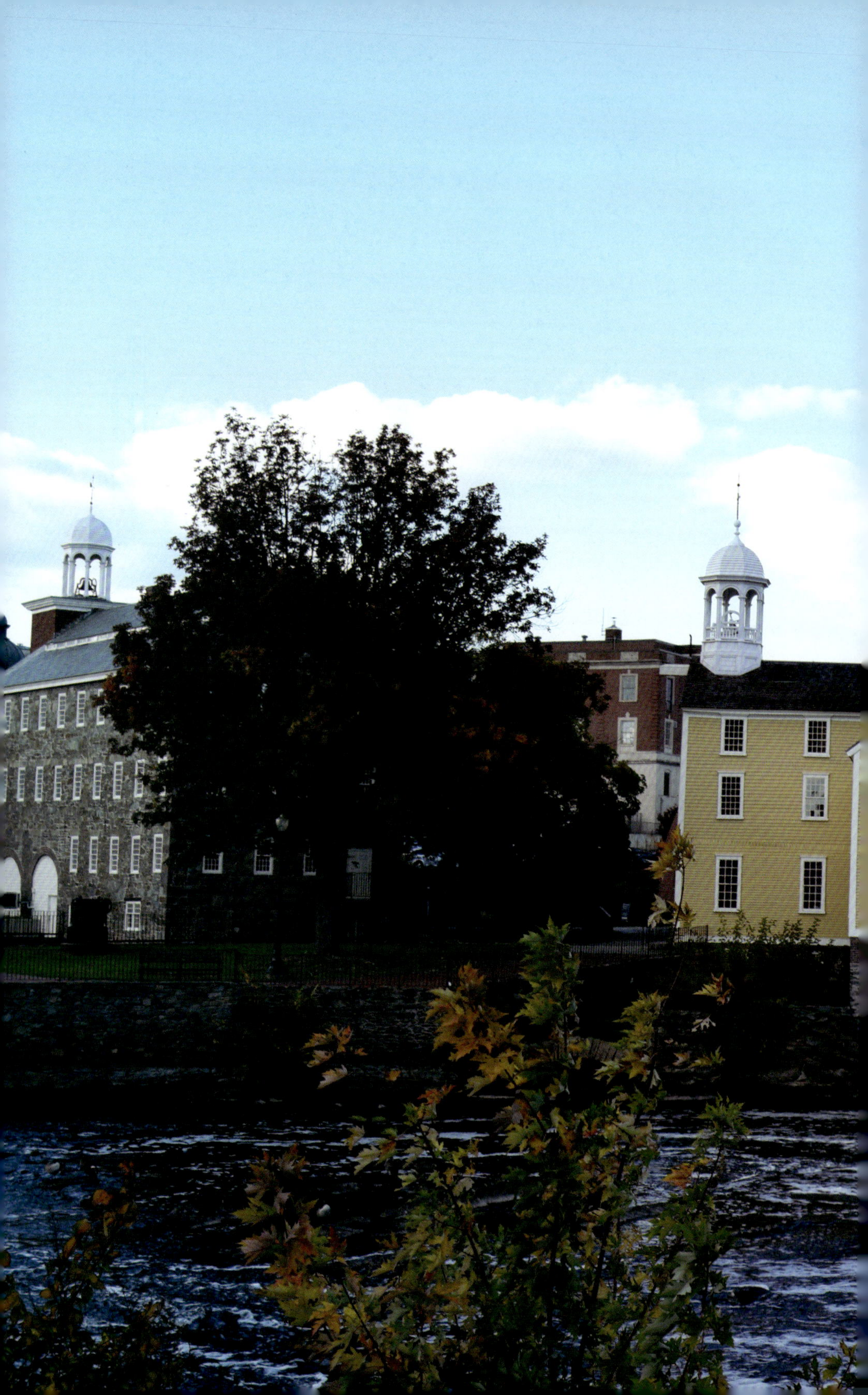

INDUSTRIAL INVENTION (page 70)

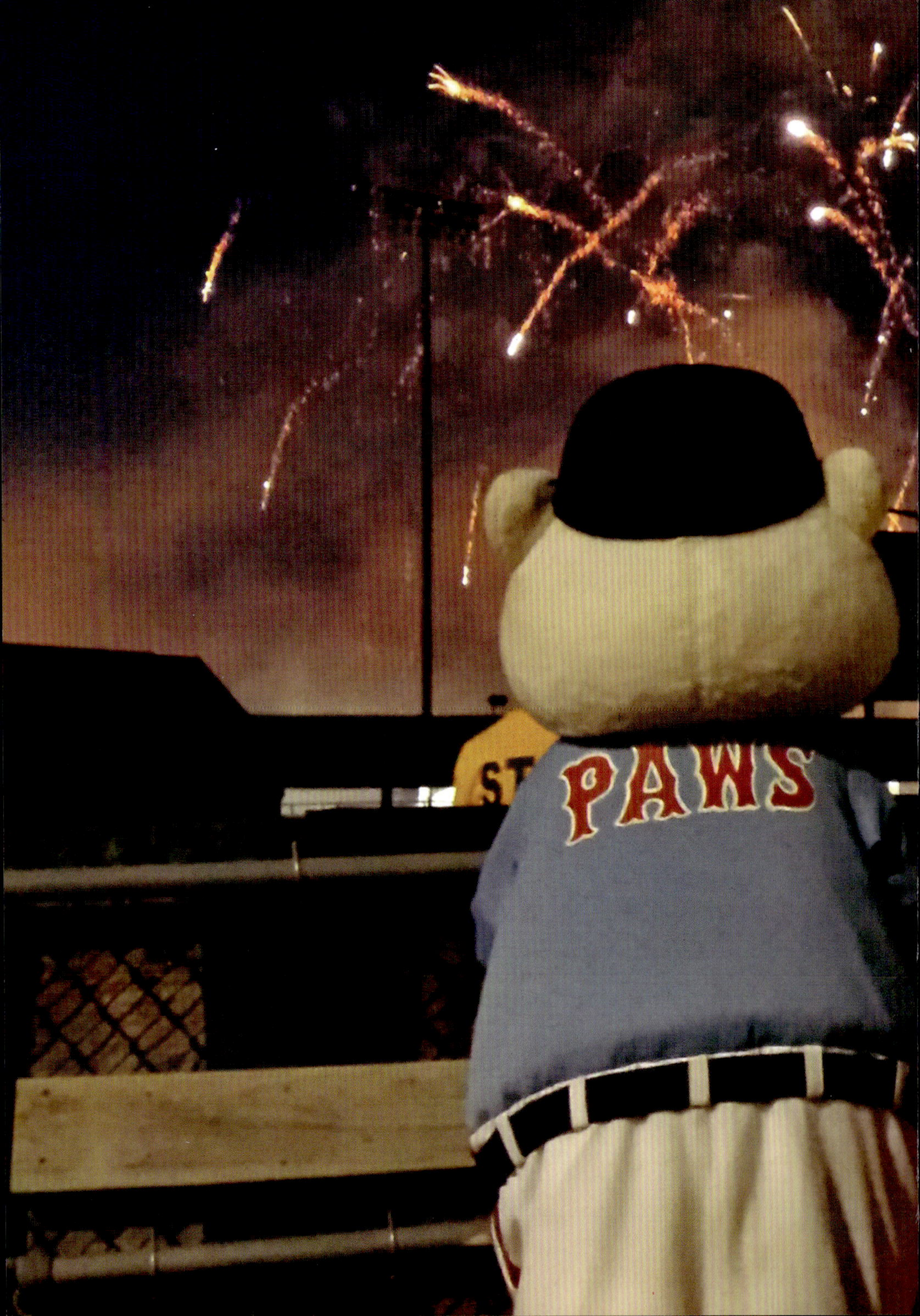
PAWS

EXTRA, EXTRA INNINGS (page 16)

VROOM, VROOM (page 44)

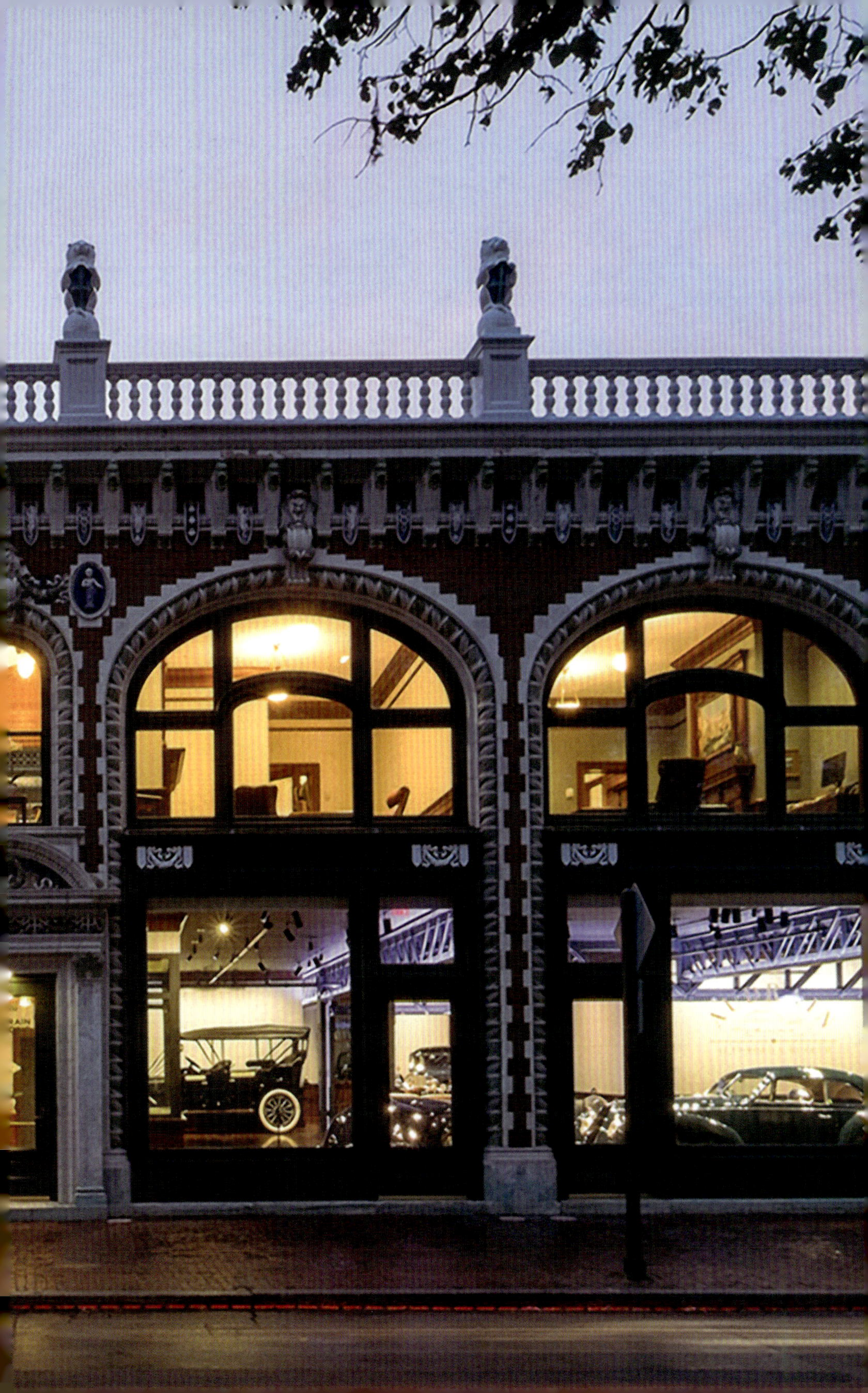

TOURO SYNAGOGUE (page 136)

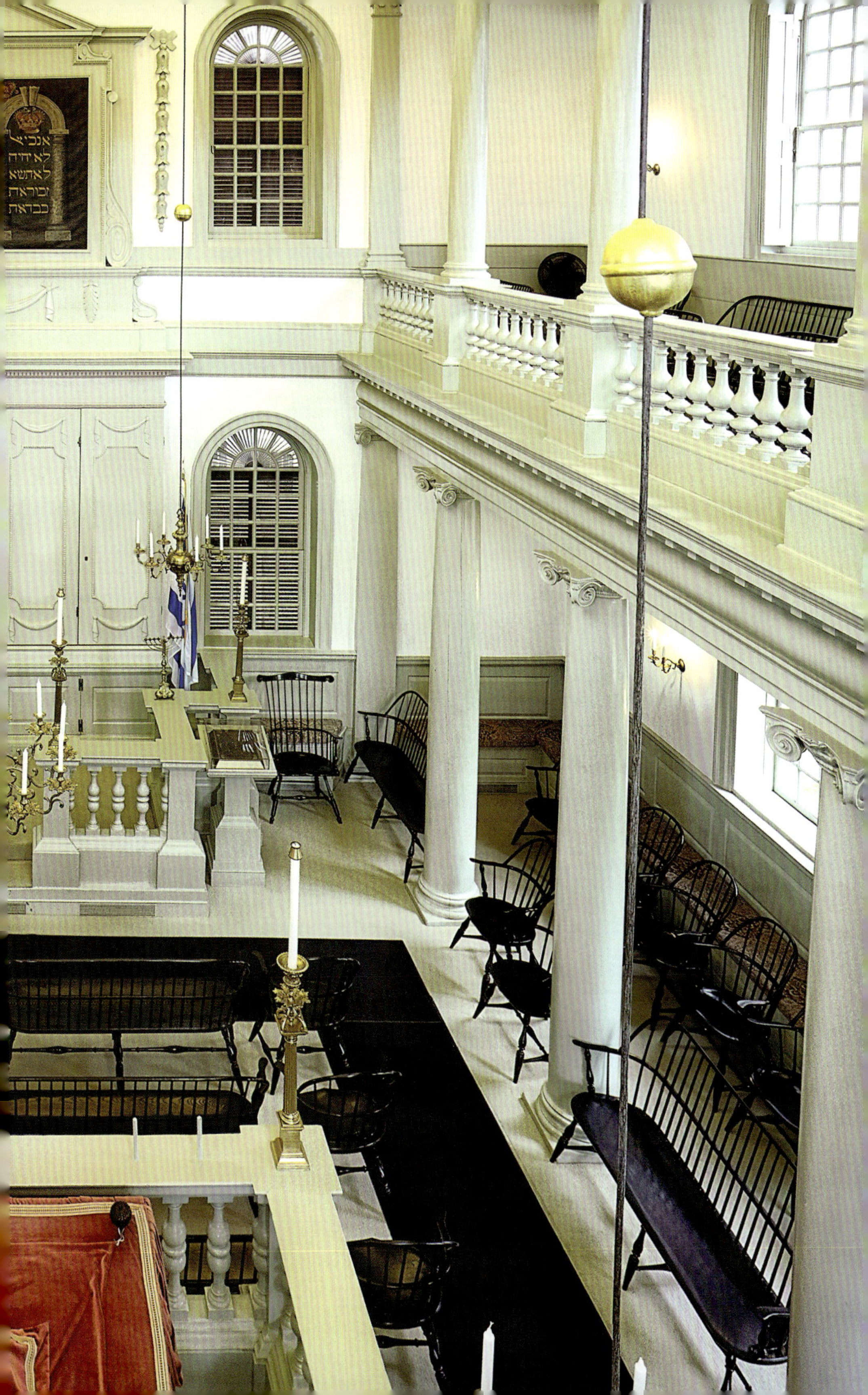
אנכי
לא יהיה
לא תשא
זכור את
כבד את

BACKSTAGE GALLERY (page 50)

PURGATORY CHASM (page 126)

DRAGON RACES (page 40)

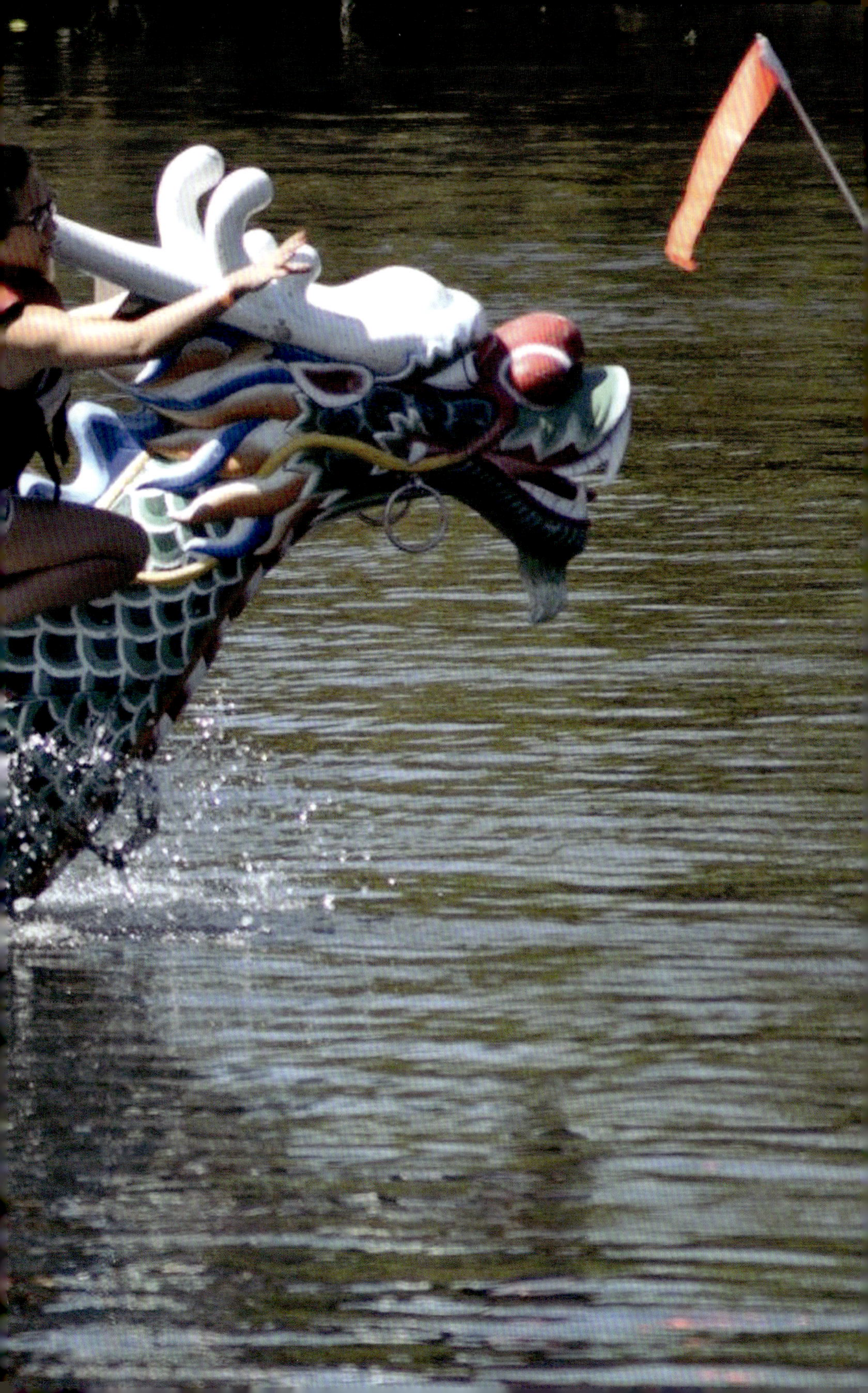

BARNABY'S CASTLE (page 36)

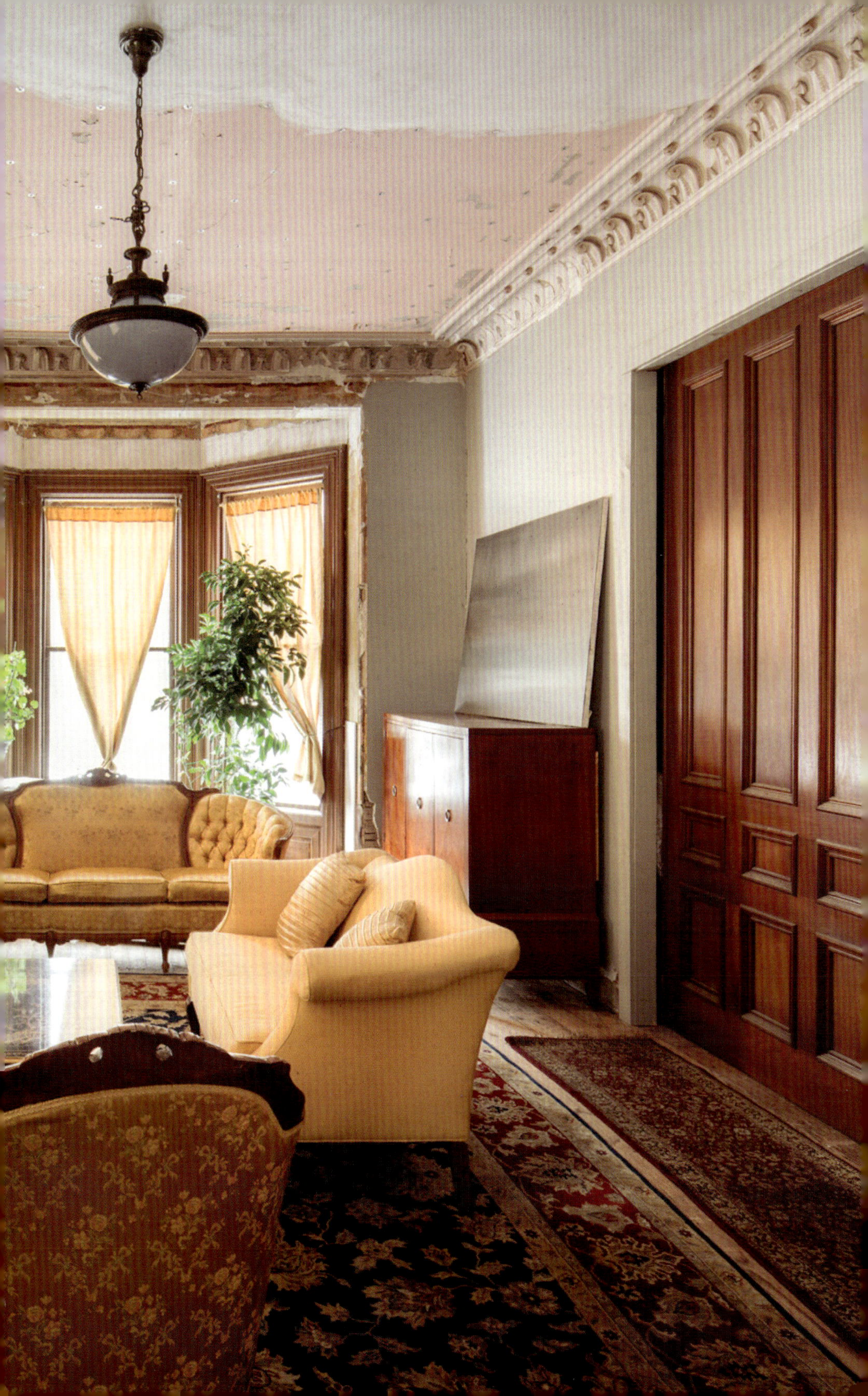

ROSE ISLAND LIGHT (page 38)

GREEN ANIMALS TOPIARY GARDEN (page 168)

44 JAILHOUSE INN

Where can you get locked up for the night and keep the key?

Repurposing former civic buildings for recreational and commercial use can have beautiful results, and Newport's Jailhouse Inn is a remarkable example. Located on historic Marlborough Street—though in a city like Newport you're never far from a piece of history—the building has been around since 1772, when it was built to replace the original 1680 city jail. During this period, jailhouses throughout post-Colonial America were not used as reformatory institutions or to house offenders but as temporary shelter for criminals moving through the system. Perhaps because it was never intended for long-term stays, the jailhouse is noted to have been easy to flee from, and many stories of escape have been documented. Use of the jail changed after an 1888 renovation, and from that time until 1986—nearly a century!—it was the Newport Police Department. When the department found a new, more modern home, the building found new life as the Jailhouse Inn. Renovated again in 2005, the jailhouse still retains elements of its former life scattered throughout, including old signage listing the various police departments it once housed. Perhaps the most significant historical element is the inn's check-in desk, which features bars once hung to separate jailhouse officials from the public. Though they aren't widely pursued or published, rumors have persisted over the years that the inn is haunted. Since there aren't any written accounts of deaths within the jail, it's purported that any hauntings are by spirits who were maligned by their time spent here in the days of public stocks and have returned to spread their ill cheer in this once quiet town.

The Jailhouse Inn in Newport was once a city jail. Some guests have reported visits from long-ago inmates.

JAILHOUSE INN

WHAT Charming Newport bed-and-breakfast, formerly a jailhouse and police department, rumored to be haunted by former inmates

WHERE 13 Marlborough St., Newport

COST Rooms start at around $200 per night

The Jailhouse Inn is a stone's throw from Newport's historic city center. Consider taking one of several walking tours offered by the Newport Historical Society to complete your city-by-the-sea experience.

45 PROVIDENCE BILTMORE HOTEL

Where is Providence's most "haunted" hotel?

It's rumored to have been the inspiration for both the Bates Motel of *Psycho* franchise fame and the Overlook Hotel of horror classic *The Shining*, but while neither notion may be true, the Providence Biltmore Hotel certainly has enough history with supposed hauntings to warrant its reputation as the city's most paranormally occupied hotel. Built in 1922, the downtown hotel has undergone several changes of ownership and extensive renovations and survived massive flooding during Hurricane Carol in 1954 to emerge as a remarkable landmark with an almost iconic façade illuminated by a beaconing red emblem. What's truly extraordinary about this hotel, which was listed on the National Register of Historic Places in 1977, is what lies inside—a stunning Art Deco lobby, stately guest rooms, an 18-floor glass elevator and, supposedly, some unhappy guests who have long missed checkout time. Visitors may encounter a wealthy patron who was tormented over losing his fortune during the Great Depression. He jumped to his death from a 14th-floor window and now continues to fall in front of the windows where hotel occupants would have witnessed his death. Other ghosts reported to be haunting the Biltmore include several who were murdered

---

If you encounter a ghost while staying at the Biltmore, don't worry. No reports have been made of any spirits harming the living—at least not yet.

The Biltmore in downtown Providence is rumored to be haunted by former guests who met an untimely death while staying there. Photo courtesy of Tony Kent via Wikimedia Commons

PROVIDENCE BILTMORE HOTEL

WHAT The city's most haunted hotel

WHERE 11 Dorrance St.

COST Rooms start at around $300 per night

there during Prohibition, when the hotel served as a hot spot for imbibing cocktails, though these spirits seem to be seeking an eternal after-party, since they are most often heard laughing. Several theories try to explain why ghosts just won't leave the hotel, with most mentioning that its construction was financed by a well-known Satanist.

46 GREAT SWAMP FIGHT MONUMENT

Where is Rhode Island's tribute to this long-forgotten battle?

King Philip's War, fought from 1675 to 1678 between Indians and English colonists and their Indian allies, nearly devastated the New England colonies—in population, economy, and settlements—and set the stage for the birth of a new nation separate and distinct from England. One of the war's deadliest battles was fought in South Kingstown, Rhode Island, about 30 miles southwest of Providence. By fall 1675, Chief Metacomet—who had adopted the name Philip—of the Massachusetts Wampanoag tribe, along with his allies, had been fighting the colonists there and in Connecticut. Rhode Island Narragansett tribe Chief Sachem had tried to remain neutral, but he would not refuse refuge to Wampanoag women, children, and the elderly, and colonists used this as justification to strike a Narragansett fort in a South Kingstown swamp. After a minor setback, Colonial forces attacked on December 19, 1675, and defeated the Narragansetts, who were forced to abandon their neutrality and join Chief Metacomet's efforts. Reports estimate the Great Swamp Fight death toll at 600 Native Americans—including women and children—who were massacred or died of wounds or exposure to the elements after they escaped into the winter's bitter cold. In comparison, about 150 Colonial fighters were either slain or wounded, with some also dying of exposure. Historians have pointed to the fight as a turning point in King Philip's War and, sadly, the native tribes never truly recovered from their losses during the war. More than 230 years later, a monument was erected at a spot believed to be the battle site, where today it serves as a somber reminder of the losses of war.

The Great Swamp Fight Memorial serves as a monument to those lost during this devastating King Philip's War battle. Photo courtesy AStoddard73 via Wikimedia Commons

GREAT SWAMP FIGHT MONUMENT

WHAT Tribute to some 700 people who died in a 1675 battle during King Philip's War

WHERE Great Swamp Monument Rd., off Rt. 2, West Kingston

COST None

The monument is about a mile-and-a-half walk from the road, which is closed to cars.

47 THE PALATINE LIGHT

Is an apparition of a ghost ship haunting Block Island?

When 240 would-be Colonial American immigrants boarded the *Princess Augusta* to set sail from Rotterdam, Netherlands, in mid-1738, they had no idea that the story of their journey would still be retold more than 270 years later—let alone be the subject of local folklore and the source of a reportedly continuous haunting near the site of their demise. The trouble aboard what came to be called The Palatine—for the German region the immigrants were from—began almost from the start of the voyage. A contaminated water supply poisoned the passengers, killing some 200 of them in addition to half the 14-member crew enroute to North America. Then, as the *Princess Augusta* grew closer to this continent, extreme weather pushed her off course—she was headed to Philadelphia—and drew her north near Block Island. A snowstorm on December 27, 1738, sealed the ship's fate, as she wrecked near the island's beautiful Mohegan Bluffs. The ship's first mate, Andrew Brook, reportedly was of the dastardly persuasion and left surviving passengers onboard while he abandoned ship with his remaining crew. What happened from there—and how Block Island residents responded—is the stuff of local legend. More reliable reports indicate that those onshore did what they could to help survivors, but rumors persist that they regularly practiced luring ships to wreck offshore to collect a bounty and that the *Princess Augusta* was no exception. Some said the ship was pushed farther out to sea to sink and rest in peace or that locals burned the vessel, while others maintained that the ship was repaired and sent on to its true destination. There are a few universally accepted truths—that survivors made it ashore, except for one woman who refused to leave, that there is no physical

The Princess Augusta *met its demise off the coast of the beautiful Mohegan Bluffs on Block Island.* Photo courtesy of Waz8 via Wikimedia Commons

THE PALATINE LIGHT

WHAT Reported apparition of a ship that wrecked off the coast of Block Island in 1738

WHERE Near Mohegan Bluffs, Block Island

COST None

evidence of the ship in the waters off the island's shore or of any bodies buried beneath a marker that stands today and reads "Palatine Graves–1738," and that ever since, residents have told tales of seeing a burning ship sail past at the wreckage site with the sounds of a woman's scream piercing the night air. These sightings are regularly reported on the Saturday between Christmas and New Year's—the week the *Princess Augusta* prematurely ended its journey.

It's hard to find a bad spot for photographs on the island, but Mohegan Bluffs provides one of the best.

48 WHITE HORSE TAVERN

Where is America's oldest still-operating tavern?

While settlers, soldiers, sailors, and many others were busy setting up shop in a colonial Newport, Rhode Island in the 1670s, they also sought a gathering place where they could keep warm by a cozy fire, discuss the day's issues, and indulge in a hearty meal and drink. And so, the tavern—predecessor to the bars and restaurants today's after-work crowds enjoy—was born of necessity as much as pleasure. The country's oldest such establishment was built in 1672 as a home at the corner of Farewell and Marlborough Streets in historic Newport and opened as a tavern a year later. For more than a hundred years after, it also served as the city's center for politics and law before Newport's Colony House was built. The White Horse Tavern was given its name by a tavern keeper, Jonathan Nichols, who inherited the business in 1730. The building was restored by The Preservation Society of Newport County during the mid-1950s. Today, the restaurant—considered by the city as the building most "typical of colonial Newport"—regularly finds itself on best-of lists for its menu, wine selection, and hard-to-believe coziness and romantic atmosphere. This is no doubt enhanced by the historic elements still present, including clapboard walls and 17th-century fireplaces that instantly transport diners back to Newport's beginnings.

The White Horse Tavern in Newport has been in continuous operation since 1673. Photo courtesy of the White Horse Tavern

WHITE HORSE TAVERN

WHAT America's oldest happy-hour spot

WHERE 26 Marlborough St., Newport

COST Dinner entrees from $22

Visiting in the off-season allows for fewer crowds and more crackling fires, just like in Colonial times.

49 BEATRICE'S ROOM

Where does the life of a mysteriously eccentric Newport artist live on?

When Beatrice Turner died a spinster in 1948 at 59 years old, nearly all 3,000 paintings that she created over her somewhat unsatisfying life were burned at the city dump. If it hadn't been for the efforts of Turner's equally eccentric neighbor, that might have been the end of her story. When one Mr. Nathan Fleischer rescued around 70 of her paintings, he reportedly became a bit obsessed with Turner's life, exhibiting her paintings for admission and attracting the attention of *Life* magazine—which in 1950 ran a photo story titled "Lonely Spinster Paints 1,000 Portraits of Herself"—and giving lectures. When a taped lecture got into the hands of Winthrop Baker, who bought the Turner family's home in 1989 to turn it into an inn, the artist's story was brought back to life in a way. Turner, the only child of a Philadelphia cotton merchant and socialite, was pulled out of art school because it was deemed inappropriate for a lady of her stature; she reportedly spent her entire adulthood stifled under the burden of not living up to society's expectations of her. There are indications that she continued to dress in Victorian garb well into the 1940s and once painted her house black, and that she was a remarkable talent whose station in life prohibited her creative growth. Baker set to right the wrong he saw in this, installing Turner's original artwork and reproductions in all the inn's rooms, holding an art exhibition there, and even publishing a book about Turner and featuring photographs of her work. Today, the most popular room at the inn—under new ownership since 2010—is Beatrice's Room, a suite featuring her artwork and door panels she painted.

Beatrice Turner is known for her self-portraits, featured in a room named for her at her former home, which is now an upscale Newport inn. Photo courtesy of Giannelli Photography

BEATRICE'S ROOM

WHAT Suite at the historic Cliffside Inn that boasts original artwork by eccentric artist and former resident Beatrice Turner

WHERE 2 Seaview Ave., Newport

COST Weekend stays approximately $400/night

It could be Beatrice's dad reportedly haungting the inn, since after his death he was propped upright to sit for a painting.

50 REVERE BELL

Where can you see the largest bell ever cast by revolutionary Paul Revere?

American patriot Paul Revere is perhaps most famous—at least outside of New England—for his infamous (though somewhat historically dramatized) ride through Lexington and Concord, Massachusetts, to warn of an impending British invasion, but he was also a silversmith, engraver, and, later in life, a bell caster who, with his sons, cast nearly 400 bells inscribed with his name. Two hundred twenty-five years later, those that remain are sought-after must-sees on many a history buff's bucket list. The bells are known to have had a distinctive tone and certainly had a part in the social structure of the early United States, since they were used for everything from signaling church services to alerting people to fires. The largest of these bells, weighing in at 2,488 pounds, is in the tower in Providence's First Unitarian Church, founded in 1723 (though the current building was constructed in the early 1800s). King's Chapel in Boston also claims the largest Revere bell, but that church's website lists it at 2,437 pounds—51 pounds less than the bell in Providence. Revere began casting bells in 1792—when he was already 57 years old (not so young for the late 1700s)—when he sought to fix the cracks in the bell at his own church, New Brick Church (now Second Church) in Boston. He became skilled at the craft (it was a new one for him at the time) and brought his sons into the business. In 1804, the business moved from Boston's historic North End to nearby Canton, Massachusetts, and it is from this foundry location that the Providence church bell was cast.

Providence's First Unitarian Church is home to the largest bell cast by revolutionist Paul Revere. Photo courtesy of Richard Boober Photography

REVERE BELL

WHAT Largest bell cast by the Revere foundry

WHERE First Unitarian Church, 1 Benevolent St., Providence

COST None

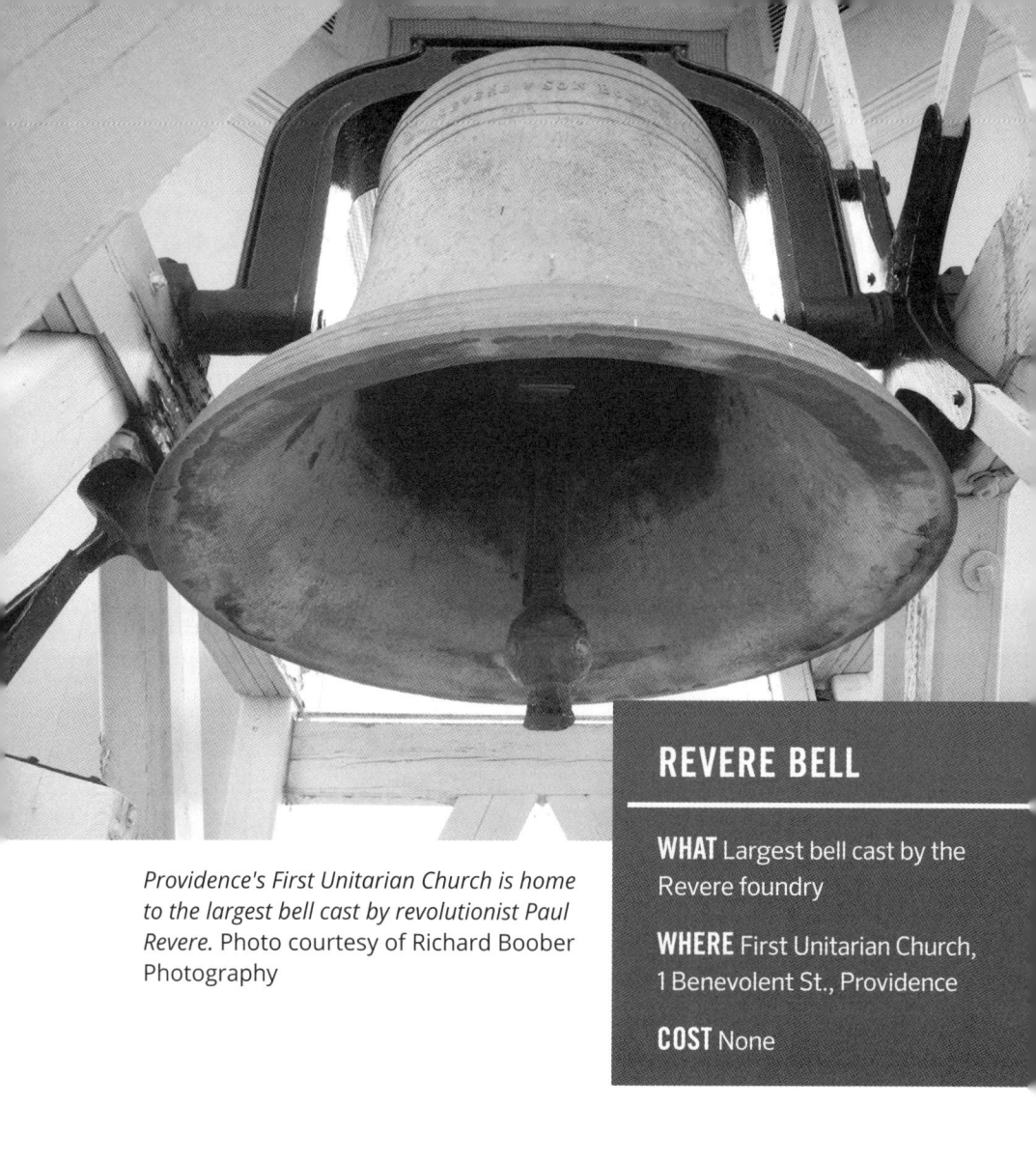

For those interested, the First Unitarian Church has quite a story all its own. Learn more by visiting www.firstunitarianprov.org

51 U-PICK 'EM

Where can you pick the prettiest tulips around from a 1700s farm?

Is a tulip farm Rhode Island's prettiest place around? That might be debatable, but visitors are in for an exquisite experience at Wicked Tulips, New England's largest u-pick tulip field. Opened in 2016, the farm has quickly become a point of pride here for its beauty, sustainability practices, and unique nature. Offering 400,000 u-pick tulips annually, visitors can select bouquets from four and a half acres of organic Holland flower bulbs, imported and planted here because they are free from pesticides that are threatening the state's—and country's—honeybee population. What flower lovers may not know is that the tulip farm occupies part of the town of Johnston's historic Snake Den Farm, established in 1789 and maintained as a working farm for more than 200 years. Snake Den Farm is part of the 744-acre Snake Den State Park, which offers some of the best fall foliage viewing in the state. Some trivia fodder related to the farm is that the owners, husband-and-wife team Jeroen and Keriann Koeman, were the only non-celebrities named among the sexiest environmentalists in the country by Rodale's *Organic Life*, a magazine that highlights natural living.

Behold the beauty of Wicked Tulips Flower Farm, a u-pick 'em flower field on a historical farm. Photo courtesy of Tammie Miller for Wicked Tulips Flower Farm

WICKED TULIPS FLOWER FARM

WHAT U-pick tulip field, the largest in New England, which is located on a historic 18th-century farm

WHERE 90 Brown Ave., Johnston

COST Tulips are $1 per stem, admission is $5

Get tickets for the season early on, so you don't risk missing out when the farm runs out of flowers.

52 NEUTACONKANUT HILL

Which hidden green space contains the city's highest point?

The nonprofit group charged with its preservation and promotion, the Neutaconkanut Hill Conservancy, calls the area Providence's last wild place, an 88-acre oasis of greenery, springs, and brooks and a natural home to deer, fox, and wild turkey that you just may encounter when visiting there. Neutaconkanut Hill, in the city's Silver Lake/Olneyville neighborhood, is often overlooked because in the city's most heavily populated area it almost seems out of place. Its quiet reputation also results from years of neglect despite a long and storied history. This neglect came to an end during the 1980s, with more recent focus placed on raising its profile as a recreational treasure. The hill's designation dates back to the state's founding in 1636, when Roger Williams and the Narragansetts made it the northwest boundary of the new Providence settlement. The Narragansett tribe reportedly held ceremonies on the hill into the 1920s. A prominent Providence family purchased some land on it in 1829 and lived there for some time. The family's last remaining heir bequeathed the land to the city in the early 1900s. The park was utilized sporatically throughout the following years—most significantly for Sunday afternoon concerts in the '30s and '40s, and visitors can see the last remains of a long-ago bandstand where they were held. More impressive will likely be the views taken in from the 296-foot summit, where you can see up to a quarter of the state and into Massachusetts.

Neutaconkanut Hill, the highest point in the city of Providence, offers unparalleled views of the city.

NEUTACONKANUT HILL

WHAT Highest point in Providence, located in a city park

WHERE Legion Memorial Dr., Providence

COST None

The conservancy offers guided hikes on the first Saturday of every month, weather permitting.

53 ST. MARY'S CHURCH

Did early Protestant Rhode Islanders put a curse on the state's first Catholic Church?

Poor Mary Doran. A 19th-century wife and mother, she most likely was trying to be an upstanding member of her community when she became the person to break ground on the state's first Catholic Church. Unfortunately for Doran, local Protestants—opposed to the establishment of a Catholic church here—cursed the first person to break ground on the building to forever lie beneath its grounds. At the time, Rhode Island was dominantly—and proudly so—Anglo-Protestants, and they were fairly intolerant of the growing Catholic population that had resulted from Irish immigrants seeking refuge from the potato famine of the 1840s. Catholics almost weren't able to build a church at all. Landowners had refused to sell them a plot until Mary and her husband, Paul, sympathizers to the cause, bought it for them. Breaking ground was a ceremonial gesture, and the church was named St. Mary's Catholic Church in 1844. Within five years, Mary and her two children—an 11-month-old girl and a 10-year-old boy—were dead. Though the likely cause was cholera, paranormal believers blamed it on the curse. Following generations always have, reporting that Mary, mostly a friendly ghost, is still there, turning lights on and off and on occasion moving items. Whether or not Mary is haunting the church, she is still there. She and her family are buried in the church's cemetery.

St. Mary's Church is rumored to be haunted by the woman who first broke ground on its construction, thanks to a Protestant curse. Photo courtesy of Swampyank via Wikimedia Commons

ST. MARY'S CHURCH

WHAT Rhode Island's oldest operating Catholic Church, thought to be haunted thanks to an 1844 Protestant curse

WHERE 70 Church St., West Warwick

COST None

Don't mention the curse to members of the parish. Haunted churches aren't something readily advertised when trying to attract new members.

125

54 PURGATORY CHASM

Is this spot hauntingly beautiful or beautifully haunted?

How you look at it will depend on what tale of local folklore you choose to believe is truly behind this striking abyss on South Beach in Middletown, Rhode Island—one is tragically glamorous and the other is anything but. Thousands of years old, the chasm was created by glaciers and has since been slowly eroded by seawater, today remaining about 10 feet wide at its peak, 120 feet long, and more than 50 feet deep. Located off Tuckerman Avenue—about 200 feet from Purgatory Avenue, you'll see a small parking area—it is accessible by a short walk off the road. Thrill seekers have reported some disappointment, as the chasm isn't large in scope, but perhaps they haven't heard the larger-than-life stories of its history. According to one legend, a young heiress with a penchant for mischief dared her suitor to express his love by leaping across the chasm, promising him her heart in return. Onto her wicked ways, the young man completed the challenge but ended their love affair, leaving her apparently so shocked that she mourned him the rest of her days. Another account tells of a perpetual haunting by an angry murderess, herself beheaded by the devil for her crime and then thrown in pieces into the chasm. Whichever local fable you follow—if you choose to follow either—the chasm is a sight to behold.

Local legend has it that a young murderess met her demise here as punishment for her wicked ways. Photo courtesy of Paul Irish: https://www.flickr.com/photos/paul_irish/159463161

PURGATORY CHASM

WHAT A 10-foot-wide chasm formed by glaciers—and surrounded by folklore

WHERE About 100 yards off Tuckerman Ave., Middletown

COST None

Behold this beautiful creation of nature, but also be careful. You don't want to fall and meet the same fate as its murderous ghost.

55 LADD SCHOOL

Is the site of a former home for the developmentally challenged and unwed mothers haunted by ghosts of those who suffered abuse at the hands of unscrupulous administrators?

While the 2015 film *Exeter* wasn't a huge commercial hit, it was successful in reigniting some conversation around a darker spot in Rhode Island's history. The thriller was filmed here on the site of the former Ladd School, a onetime home for intellectually and developmentally challenged children and young adults as well as unwed mothers, which for much of its existence was misrun—and run rampant with rumors (and some verified cases) of mistreatment of its residents. When it was founded in 1908 as the Rhode Island School for the Feeble-Minded, it was an extension of a Massachusetts institution, and its first director, Dr. Joseph Ladd, eventually tried to turn around its practice of essentially hiding away those deemed "inferior" to the rest of society. Overcrowding and poor financial backing continually made conditions worse at the school, renamed the Dr. Joseph H. Ladd School, well into the 1950s—a severely disabled nine-year-old child died at the school from suffocation, reportedly at the hands of a 20-year-old inmate. In the 1970s, its deplorable conditions were finally made public thanks to a state investigation, exposing, among other problems, several patient deaths caused by medical malpractice. As most of the country adopted deinstitutionalization to address the needs of these schools' populations, the Ladd School's necessity became less prominent, and in 1993 its last residents were relocated. Since then, its former grounds—most of the buildings have been demolished—have been

The former Ladd School, a home for the disabled that shuttered in the early 1990s, is rumored to be haunted by mistreated and murdered residents.

LADD SCHOOL

WHAT Former institution for the "feeble-minded," rumored to be haunted by mistreated and murdered residents

WHERE 162 Main St., Exeter

COST None

a point of fascination for some, including at least one set of filmmakers. *Exeter* tells the story of a vengeful child abandoned at an insane asylum, highlighted by demonic possession. Naturally, rumors of haunting by murdered and neglected patients at the school remain.

There isn't too much left of the original school to see. Those who appreciate the history of the eerie will most enjoy a visit to this spot.

129

56 ROSE FERRON'S GRAVE

Was a Rhode Island woman plagued by illness really a stigmatist?

Among those lying in eternal rest in the Precious Blood Cemetery in Woonsocket is Rose Ferron, a Rhode Island woman who died in 1936 when she was only 33 years old after a near lifetime full of pain and illness. But was Little Rose something more? One of 10 children born to Catholic Canadian immigrants, Ferron was a reported stigmatist—a person bearing stigmata, or body marks or painful sensations resembling the crucifixion wounds of Jesus Christ. It's written that after receiving her first vision of Jesus at just six years old, Little Rose was stricken with an enigmatic paralysis that eventually left her bedridden. In adulthood, she was said to have had visible stigmata, including a crown of thorns, that would appear weekly on Fridays during Lent. These marks attracted the attention of religious devotees, who regularly visited her bedside until she passed away, dying at the same age as Jesus Christ at his death. Believers cannot be shaken in their assertion that Rose was indeed a stigmatist, with varied reports of "miracles" attributed to her posthumously, though an inquiry into her life was abandoned by the Catholic Church in the 1960s. The Rose Ferron Foundation of Rhode Island seeks to inform the public about the sacrifice of "La Petite Rose" for Christ and her fellow Catholics.

It is reported that Rose was the only stigmatist ever to reside in New England.

Believers say former Rhode Islander Rose Ferron was a stigmatist who reportedly bore body marks resembling the crucifixion wounds of Jesus Christ. Photo courtesy of the Rose Ferron Society of Rhode Island

ROSE FERRON GRAVE

WHAT Burial site of a reported stigmatist

WHERE Precious Blood Cemetery, Diamond Hill Rd.

COST None

57 V-J DAY

What ties does Rhode Island have to a largely unobserved holiday?

It is a source of both contention and confusion among many Rhode Islanders that the smallest state in the union is also the only one to still observe V-J Day, or Victory over Japan Day, the day Japan surrendered—and essentially brought to an end—World War II. On August 14, 1945, (which was August 15 in Japan), Americans across the country celebrated with well-deserved revelry—perhaps most famously, at least in photographs, in Times Square, New York—that years of fighting and suffering were at last over. Celebrations dwindled over the years due to growing sentiment that festivities were offensive because Japan became one of America's strongest allies and disrespectful to Japanese-Americans because of the nuclear bombings of Hiroshima and Nagasaki. Rhode Island continues to observe the holiday on the second Monday of August. While attempts in the 1980s and 1990s to eliminate the holiday failed, the state General Assembly passed a resolution that "Victory Day is not a day to express satisfaction in the destruction and death caused by nuclear bombs at Hiroshima and Nagasaki" to refocus commemoration for Rhode Islanders who fought in the Pacific theater during the war. Unrelated to the V-J Day celebration controversy, in 2012 Newport resident George Mendosa was identified as the sailor in the famous *V-J Day in Times Square* photograph taken by *Life* photographer Alfred Eisenstaedt.

A 2012 book identified a Rhode Islander as the kissing sailor from the famous V-J Day in Times Square *photograph taken by* Life *photographer Alfred Eisenstaedt.* Photo courtesy of U.S. Navy

V-J DAY

WHAT Holiday observed in August that commemorates Rhode Islanders who fought in the Pacific theater during World War II

WHERE N/A

COST None

Many Rhode Islanders have this day off from work. If your plans involve tickets or reservations, make them early.

133

58 BRISTOL FOURTH OF JULY PARADE

How did the country come to have a parade for its birthday?

When you're one of the oldest states in the country, there's bound to be a lot of firsts to boast about. Bristol's Fourth of July celebration is no exception, since it holds the title of the country's longest-operating July 4th parade. The celebration began with a much less celebratory name: Patriotic Exercises. Starting after the Revolutionary War in 1785, town citizens came together—through a procession to the gathering spot—to honor veterans who had fought in the war and fallen soldiers who had given their lives to establish the new nation and to celebrate a new era of independence from Great Britain. The effort was spearheaded by war veteran Rev. Henry Wight of the First Congregational Church. An annual celebration has been held every year since, giving Bristol bragging rights and a nickname as America's most patriotic town. Today, the celebration begins on June 14—Flag Day—and features several events, including a concert series, a 4th of July Ball, and a Drum Corps show. Annual festivities conclude with the Military, Civic and Firemen's Parade, which itself starts with the Patriotic Exercises, featuring a patriotic speaker that many times has been a First Congregational Church leader. The famous parade regularly attracts some 200,000 visitors.

Bristol's Fourth of July festivities include the longest continually operating parade in the United States, begun in 1785. Photo courtesy of Kenneth Zirkel via Wikimedia Commons

BRISTOL 4TH OF JULY CELEBRATION

WHAT The country's oldest still-operating 4th of July parade

WHERE Bristol

COST Parade watching is free

Bristol is a beautiful place to visit, featuring several Gilded Age mansions and fine dining for any taste.

135

59 TOURO SYNAGOGUE

How did Rhode Island come to house the country's first—and still in service—synagogue?

Newport's Jewish population made history when it opened the country's first synagogue in December 1763, but, as it probably stands for all firsts accomplished in this country, they likely couldn't have anticipated the wonder with which people would look back at the event more than 250 years later. Building the synagogue, work of architectural art that it is, was born out of necessity. The first Jewish residents came to Newport around 1700, arriving from Barbados, and formed a congregation that by the mid-1700s had grown large enough to need an official house of worship. Merchant Peter Harrison designed the synagogue without any practical education or experience in the trade. It's likely that he borrowed ideas from existing synagogues and is credited with being an early adapter of the European Palladian style, which he also applied to the city's Redwood Library (the country's oldest community library still in its original building). The synagogue did not operate during the American Revolution, when most of Newport's Jews fled the British occupation. An exception was Isaac Touro, who stayed behind as caretaker when the building was used as a British hospital. Although British troops burned many Newport structures, the synagogue was deemed useful to their needs. When the city's Jewish population dwindled after the war, the synagogue was opened only for special services and occasions—and used as a burial site—but was reopened due to a population resurgence in the late 1880s. Touro Synagogue was officially named in the 1820s after Isaac Touro's sons, who left money in their wills to ensure the synagogue's continued maintenance. The synagogue

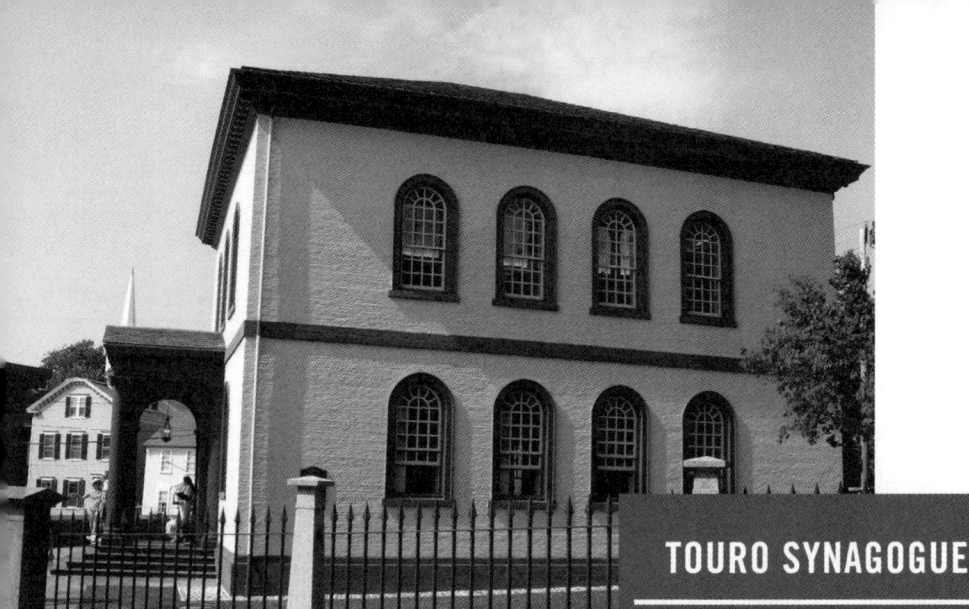

Located in Newport, Touro Synagogue is the nation's oldest synagogue. Photo courtesy of Swampyank via Wikimedia Commons

TOURO SYNAGOGUE

WHAT Oldest synagogue in the United States

WHERE 72 Touro St., Newport

COST Adults, $12; seniors, $10; students and members of the military, $8; children age 13 and under, free

remains open today as a place of worship and for tours that highlight its historical and architectural significance. A special ceremony is held each year for the reading of George Washington's letter to former congregation president Moses Mendes Seixas. The letter, sent in response to Seixas, included support of religious freedom.

Tours are not offered on Jewish holidays, so be sure to check the synagogue's calendar.

60 NECRONOMICON

Where is the weirdest festival of them all?

Fans of famed 20th-century horror writer H. P. Lovecraft—perhaps Providence's most beloved literary genius—will find no better place to celebrate his work and legacy, meet fellow admirers, and have a downright weirdly good time than at NecronomiCon Providence. The biennial festival is run by the Lovecraft Arts & Sciences Council, a Providence-based national nonprofit organization that also runs a storefront inside the historic Arcade downtown. The council serves year-round as a "networking center" for those interested in the world of weird literature, from scholars to authors and avid readers. NecronomiCon Providence is its signature event and functions as a convention with panel discussions on various topics, including historic weird fiction and creating short horror films; lots of gaming; a marketplace; and the Armitage Symposium, which focuses on showcasing academic works related to the horror fiction and weird art genres. The convention takes its name from an element of Lovecraft's work. The Necronomicon is seen throughout the author's stories as a grimoire (textbook of magic) and was first mentioned in a 1924 short story titled "The Hound." The Necronomicon is almost as notorious as Lovecraft himself, with many fans believing it to be an actual book. It's reported that Lovecraft once said the name "Necronomicon" came to him in a dream.

Gaming is a popular activity at NecronomiCon Providence, a four-day biennial conference dedicated to the work and life of H. P. Lovecraft and other authors and scholars of weird fiction. Photos courtesy of Necronomicon Providence

NECRONOMICON

WHAT Festival celebrating weird fiction, its creators, and their legacies, including famed 20th-century Providence author H. P. Lovecraft, held every two years, usually in August

WHERE Festival activities are held at various venues throughout Providence

COST 2017 festival tickets were priced starting at $80

Not in town during the festival? Visit the Lovecraft Arts & Sciences storefront inside the Arcade Building downtown to shop all things Lovecraft and NecronomiCon.

61 TEMPLE TO MUSIC

Is this serene spot inside Roger Williams Park Rhode Island's quietest place?

Can one of the most popular places for outdoor concerts and entertainment at the same time be the best spot in Rhode Island for quiet reflection? The answer is yes, just perhaps not at the exact same time. Nestled inside Roger Williams Park is the Temple to Music—first named the Benedict Monument to Music—a magnificent structure constructed of Vermont maple and dedicated in 1924 as a gift from a local olive oil merchant. This was about half a century after the park was donated to the city of Providence by Betsey Williams, the last great-great-great-granddaughter of state founder Roger Williams. The land had housed the family farm and was the last parcel the family still owned from his original pact with the Narragansett tribe when he arrived here in 1636. Visitors to the park can see the Betsey Williams Cottage standing today as well as the Williams family burial ground. The park itself, which borders the city of Cranston, was constructed in the 1880s. It addition to the Temple to Music, it houses visitor must-sees such as the Roger Williams Park Zoo and the Roger Williams Park Botanical Center.

The Temple to Music at Roger Williams Park is a quiet retreat. Photo courtesy of Rhododendrites via Wikimedia Commons

TEMPLE TO MUSIC

WHAT Temple within Roger Williams Park, a favored spot for outdoor concerts and at other times considered the quietest place in the state

WHERE Roger Williams Park, 1000 Elmwood Ave., Providence

COST None

Roger Williams Park is worth a day trip for all there is to explore and makes for a great family-fun venue.

62 FORT ADAMS

Where can you bunk down where Civil War soldiers once slept?

One of the largest forts in the country, Fort Adams in Newport was established in 1799 and named for then-sitting President John Adams. (The current building was built between 1824 and 1857.) The fort housed military operations as well as officers and their families for various purposes during the War of 1812, the Civil War, the Spanish-American War, World War I, and World War II. As its website boasts, not one "shot in anger" was fired from the fort. During the Civil War, the U.S. Navy became concerned that its Annapolis, Maryland, headquarters were compromised by Southern sympathizers and moved the Naval Academy to Fort Adams. In 1953, the U.S. Army gave ownership of the fort to the U.S. Navy, and the fort and its land were given to the state of Rhode Island in 1965. The fort was declared a National Historic Landmark in 1976, and the Fort Adams Trust, which today gives guided tours here, was formed in 1994. Public tours were first offered in the 1970s but were canceled until the trust took over due to state budget cuts. (The PBS movie *The Scarlet Letter* was filmed here during the initial tour period.) Public tours include visits to officers' quarters and education about the fort's history and planned restorations as well as a tour of the underground tunnels. Overnight tours—advertised as ideal for scout and school groups—allow visitors to sleep in soldiers' bunkrooms.

Fort Adams, in Newport, offers visitors the chance to see the inner workings of a once-active military fort. Photo courtesy of Ad Meskens via Wikimedia Commons

FORT ADAMS

WHAT Former U.S. Army post in Newport dating to 1799 and now available for tours

WHERE 90 Fort Adams Dr., Newport

COST Adults, $12; children ages 6–17, $6; children ages 5 and under, free

---

The fort lays claim to being the best sunset-watching spot in Newport, with a two-and-a-half-mile loop around Fort Adams State Park giving views of Newport Harbor and the Newport Bridge.

65 SOUTHERNMOST SCHOOL HOUSE

Why is the nation's oldest one-room schoolhouse a hidden treasure?

Its story is remarkable—another first for Rhode Island, in this case a claim as the oldest still-standing one-room schoolhouse in the United States—but it's easy to see why the Portsmouth schoolhouse remains largely unknown. Its location today in the pretty town of Portsmouth all but hides it from public view. Nestled on East Main Road, it's nearly obscured by its surroundings—including the Portsmouth Historical Society, which maintains the building. It's the second of two schoolhouses built in the early 1700s in Portsmouth, making it not the oldest one-room schoolhouse ever built in the United States but the oldest still standing. The town commissioned the buildings in 1725, and the still-standing Southernmost Schoolhouse was constructed for $100 in today's dollars to serve approximately 20 students. It was moved from its original location around 1800 and in 1863—after a new town school was built—was auctioned off and then used as a harness shed. It was donated to the Portsmouth Historical Society in 1952. Visitors will see several inscriptions on its walls—the most identifiable being a math equation—and an original student desk, carefully preserved. Its still-standing status is somewhat of an anomaly. Most one-room schoolhouses built and used during the same time period are no longer standing because they were torn down for newer, larger facilities as town populations grew.

The nation's oldest one-room schoolhouse still stands in Portsmouth, Rhode Island. Photo courtesy of Swampyank via Wikimedia Commons

SOUTHERNMOST SCHOOL HOUSE

WHAT The nation's oldest one-room schoolhouse

WHERE 870 East Main Rd., Portsmouth

COST None

Stop by the Portsmouth Historical Museum, which offers rotating exhibits curated around local interests.

66. CAREY MANSION

Where can you spy the *Dark Shadows* mansion?

The city of Newport, Rhode Island, is well known the world over for its famous Gilded Age mansions, which allow visitors a glimpse into grander times, but the city also boasts several historic homes that aren't on the tourist circuit. One such home is Seaview Terrace, also known as the Carey Mansion, a privately owned residence that's also the city's fifth-largest mansion. The mansion was completed in 1925, after Washington, D.C., millionaire Edson Bradley moved his Dupont Circle mansion—known as Aladdin's Palace—here, incorporating his dismantled home into an existing property named Seaview. Bradley designed his new mansion in the French Renaissance Revival Châteauesque style, using elements built in France 20 years before and featuring turrets, stained glass windows, and doorways with high arches. After Bradley's death in 1935, his daughter lived there until 1941. After being used by the U.S. Army for officer housing during World War II, it housed an all-girl boarding school and was then leased to Newport's Salve Regina University, which utilized it for dormitory space and as a music hall, among other functions, until 2009. It's been known as the Carey Mansion since 1974, when a New York

---

Since the house is privately owned, photographers should take care to be respectful in keeping a safe distance when taking pictures.

The Carey Mansion, seen here in its heyday and now closed to the public, rose to pop culture prominence as the Dark Shadows *castle.* Photo courtesy of Jim McCullars via Wikimedia Commons

CAREY MANSION

WHAT Private Newport mansion—official name Seaview Terrace—that was used as the exterior for the mansion in the hit TV show *Dark Shadows*

WHERE 207 Ruggles Ave., Newport

COST None

family purchased the home. It was one of the last grand houses built in Newport during a period when wealthy Americans—many of them occupying elevated positions in society—constructed summer homes here. The mansion rose to prominent pop culture status when it was used for exterior shots of the family home during the airing of the TV soap opera *Dark Shadows*—the supernatural drama about the eerie Collins family, featuring the infamous Barnabas Collins—on ABC from 1966 to 1971.

67 FORT WETHERILL

Where can you go scuba diving where American forces were once housed during the American Revolution?

In the late 1700s, Fort Wetherill, on Conanicut Island in scenic Jamestown, was a popular choice for social outings, which is still true today, but there's a lot more to the story than that of a pretty recreational spot. In its 240-year history, the fort has been a defense point for forces during the American Revolution and both world wars, has served as artistic inspiration, and housed a tramway system (the tracks are still intact) to transport mines to and from the island in war time. Fort Wetherill was built in 1899 on what was Fort Dumpling—which was constructed in 1776 and housed American, British, and French fighters during the American Revolution—and was named for Jamestown native Capt. Alexander Macomb Wetherill, who was killed during the Battle of San Juan Hill, a pivotal battle of the Spanish-American War. The fort assisted American efforts during World War I and during World War II served as, among other things, a training center for German prisoners of war. Post-World War II, it was abandoned until the state of Rhode Island acquired it in 1972 and turned it into a state park. Today, it's a relaxation destination for picnics, picture taking, fishing, bird watching, walking—and scuba diving—and is open sunrise to sunset. It's also quite a popular spot for graffiti, though this is not advised except for photographing by urban explorers.

FORT WETHERILL

WHAT Former artillery fort, now a reservation area and recreation spot for scuba diving, among other things

WHERE 3 Fort Wetherill Rd., Jamestown

COST None

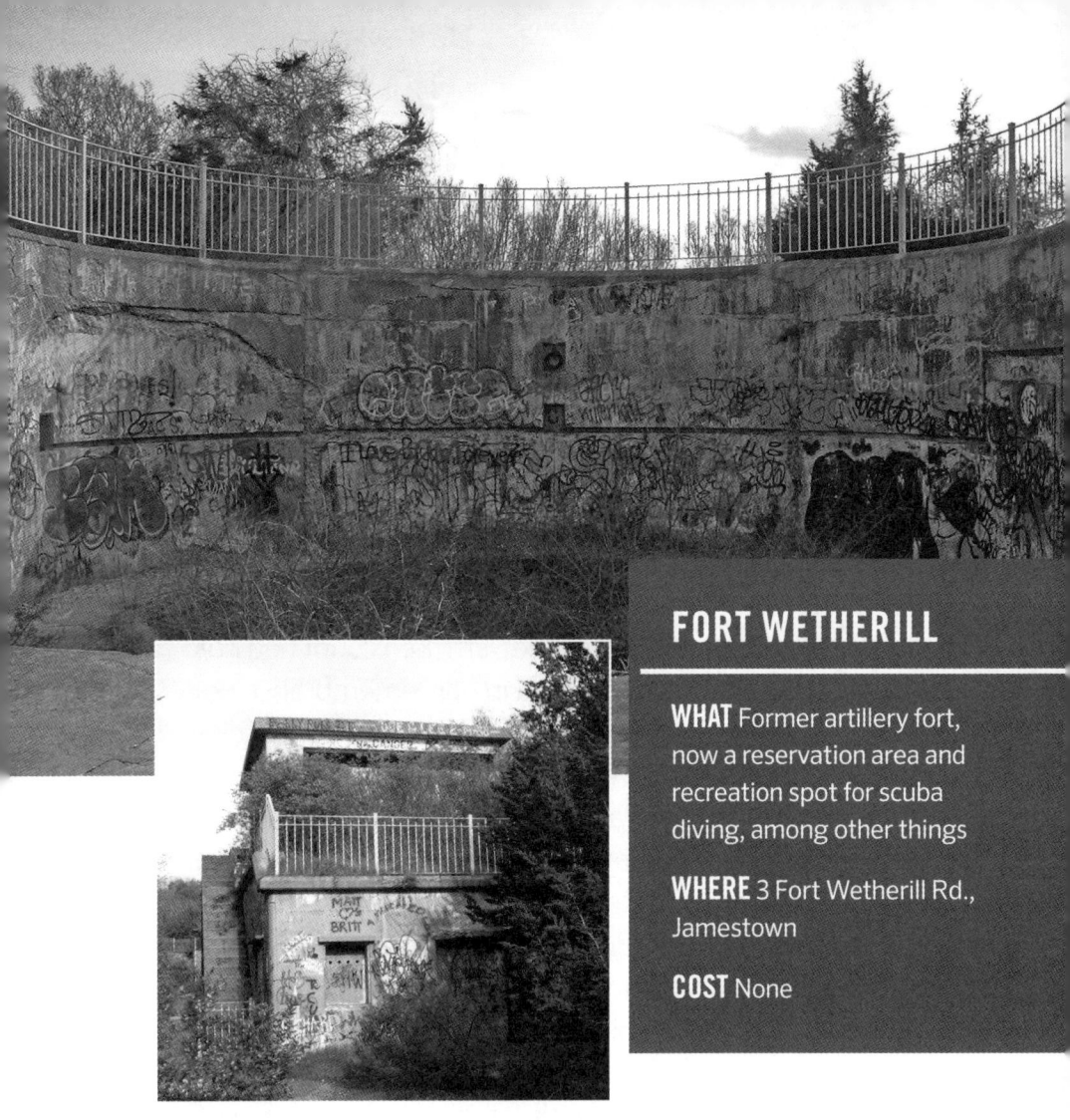

Visitors to Fort Wetherill, built in the late 1800s and used during both world wars, is also a spot for scuba diving in Jamestown. Photo courtesy of Rhododendrites (1) and Swampyank (2) via Wikimedia Commons

The fort is a great viewing spot for the Tall Ships America event that happens each summer in Narragansett Bay and Newport's America's Cup sailing races.

68. CARRIE AND THE COUNT

Who's telling this wonderful love story?

Rhode Island Monthly has called it "the greatest love story never told," and one Providence restaurateur and historian has devoted his eatery's Valentine's Day to honoring it. Carrie Mathilde Brown, granddaughter of Brown University namesake Nicholas Brown Jr., married Italian diplomat Count Paul Bajnotti (of Turin, Italy) in 1876. Though the couple resided in Italy, their ties to Providence remained throughout the marriage. So strong were these ties that when Carrie died in 1896, the grief-stricken count had not one but three memorials erected in her remembrance not in Italy but here in Providence—the Carrie Tower at Brown University, the Carrie Brown Bajnotti Memorial Fountain at Burnside Park, and the Pancratiast statue at Roger Williams Park. The fountain is quite remarkable, with a granite basin housing 234 spray outlets and a statue featuring the Angel of Life fighting off the confines of duty, passion, and greed. The tower at Brown University features a clock that no longer tolls, but Robert Burke, an expert on the city and the owner of Pot au Feu, a downtown French restaurant once loved by Julia Child is working to change that, in part with an annual history dinner held around Valentine's Day that includes a retelling of the couple's tale. One part of the legacy that did not last was Bajnotti's establishment of a dowry that would have funded marriage for a "young woman of virtue" here. The city did not accept his proposal.

CARRIE MATHILDE BROWN TRIBUTES

WHAT Three monuments erected in memory of Carrie Mathilde Brown, a member of a prominent Providence family, by her husband, an Italian count

WHERE Brown University, Burnside Park, and Roger Williams Park

COST None

One of three monuments to former Providence socialite Carrie Mathilde Brown can be found on the Brown University campus. The university was named for her grandfather, Nicholas Brown Jr. Photo courtesy of Ad Meskens via Wikimedia Commons

Even if you aren't in town on Valentine's Day, dining at Pot au Feu is one of the most pleasurable culinary experiences to be had in the city.

69 BLUE VIOLET

Why is this pretty flower a Rhode Island state symbol?

As it turns out, a flower by any other name really isn't the same—at least in Rhode Island. In 1897, state school children voted to name the common meadow violet the state flower instead of several other flowers, including the buttercup, daisy, pansy, and rose. Records from the time indicate that residents believed they were adopting the *Viola pedata*—the bird foot violet—as the state flower, but by the time state officials got around to signing the notion into law, this violet was extremely hard to find blooming on Rhode Island land, and in 1968 the official state flower was recorded as the *Viola palmata*, or wood violet. State manuals, however, showed images of the *Viola sororia*, the common blue violet. In the late 1980s, the newly formed Rhode Island Wild Plant Society decided the state flower confusion needed to be cleared up once and for all, and in July 2001 the common blue violet emerged victorious. Characterized by either a snow white or blue-purple color and heart-shaped leaves that grow on separate stems, the flower reaches its blooming peak from April through June and is also the state flower of Illinois, New Jersey, and Wisconsin.

The common blue violet is a natural source of vitamins A and C and can be used for cake decoration.

Rhode Island's official state flower is the pretty blue violet. Photo courtesy of U.S. Fish and Wildlife Service

COMMON BLUE VIOLET

WHAT Rhode Island State Flower

WHERE Most commonly found from Warwick to the state's northern border

COST None

70 STEPHEN HOPKINS

Who was Rhode Island's "greatest statesman"?

Stephen Hopkins, a Rhode Island native, might best be remembered as one of the two delegates to the First Continental Congress where, in 1776, he signed the Declaration of Independence for Rhode Island. Add his other notable accomplishments—serving as governor, a Chief Justice of the Rhode Island Supreme Court, and early backer and first chancellor of what is now Brown University—and it's easy to see why he's considered the state's "greatest statesman." It's also well noted that he teamed with Benjamin Franklin to advocate for the union as a delegate to the Congress of Albany and that he published *The Rights of Colonies Examined*, which denounced the Stamp Act. One of his lesser-known political accomplishments was penning what became one of the country's first antislavery laws. He introduced a 1774 bill that abolished the importation of slaves into the colony, following his second marriage to a Quaker woman whose religion admonished the practice, but that likely wasn't the only reason. It's well documented that Hopkins firmly believed slavery was against God's will, and that two of his slaves lived at least somewhat independently for years before his death. At one point, he saw fit to include in his will provisions that his slaves, upon his death, would be treated in a way that guaranteed them a satisfying life. It is worth noting, however, that Hopkins was not universal in this—he also noted that his female slave would not be granted emancipation because she needed to fulfill motherly duties. Even though Hopkins's measure was probably at least somewhat influenced by the fact that the slave trade in the New England colonies was not profitable, it's still a remarkable measure of a remarkable man.

Stephen Hopkins, a signer of the Declaration of Independence, was also an early opposer of slavery. Though he owned several, he introduced a bill barring importation of slaves into the Rhode Island Colony, one of the country's first antislavery laws, in 1774. Photo courtesy of English Wikipedia via Wikimedia Commons

STEPHEN HOPKINS

WHAT The home of Rhode Island's greatest statesman, a governor, chief justice of the Rhode Island Supreme Court, signer of the Declaration of Independence, and author of one of the country's first antislavery bills

WHERE 15 Hopkins St., Providence

COST Admittance is free; donations accepted

As a bonus, his residence features a bedchamber where George Washington once slept.

71 CUMBERLANDITE

Where in Rhode Island is the only place in the world where you can find this magnetic rock?

When your state is the only place you can find something, it's worth giving that something symbolic status. Cumberlandite, an "uncommon mafic igneous rock known as a troctolite," is Rhode Island's State Rock and can be found in large quantities only in a four-acre wooded area off Elder Ballou Meeting House Road in Cumberland, just a few miles outside Providence. (Smaller amounts have been documented throughout the Narragansett Bay watershed, which runs for 147 miles on Rhode Island Sound's north side). Black in color, the rock contains a large amount of iron—mixed with other minerals—making it slightly magnetic and unusual. Records indicate the rock was discovered by early Rhode Island settlers and was considered useful in manufacturing cannons and farm tools as late as the nineteenth century, but actual efforts to use it to make cannons during the Revolutionary War proved futile because the iron content in the rock was actually too weak. Nearby the rock's main home, the Ballou graveyard contains tombstones made from Cumberlandite.

Cumberlandite, Rhode Island's state rock, is so rare it is found in large quantities in only one spot in the state. Photo courtesy of James St. John: https://www.flickr.com/photos/jsjgeology/14817999769

CUMBERLANDITE

WHAT Rhode Island State Rock, found in large quantities in only one location

WHERE Elder Ballou Meeting House Rd., Cumberland

COST None

When you see the Ballou graveyard on Elder Ballou Meeting House Road, park on the right shoulder, and access a dirt trail across the road. Follow the path about a hundred yards to find the Cumberlandite site.

72 AN EPIC FOOD FIGHT

What local appetizer is so good that Rhode Island became the only state to have an official one?

Was it tactical or frivolous? In 2014, the Rhode Island State Legislature put an end to the debate over naming calamari—made Rhode Island style—the official state appetizer here. A state representative named Joseph McNamara proposed the measure because he felt it would help the state support and promote its fishing and tourism industries. Supporters agreed, touting the state's majority stake in East Coast squid fishing and unique spin on the dish. Here, calamari are fried or sautéed breaded squid served with hot peppers. Critics said the move was somewhat trivial and that lawmakers should focus on moves that would do more to boost the state's economy. Others still wanted to see clams casino take the honor, as it reportedly was created at a casino here. Calamari prevailed, and while Rhode Island became the first state to put a legislative signifier next to an appetizer, giving food an official state designation is not unusual. Many states place special significance on foods or dishes that have either originated in or have become synonymous with their region. A few even have official snacks and that's also true for Rhode Island, which has an official drink (coffee milk) and state shell (quahog). The final review on this dish debate is that no matter its importance as a branding tool, it's simply delicious.

Rhode Islanders love their calamari, prepared here with hot peppers, so much that they made it the first official state appetizer in the country.

CALAMARI

WHAT Rhode Island's official state appetizer: squid breaded and then fried or sautéed and served with hot peppers

WHERE Various locations

COST Depends on the restaurant

For what the author deems the state's best, try either the Aurora Civic Association on Broadway or Hemenway's on South Main Street, both in Providence.

73 SWAN POINT CEMETERY

What stories lie beneath this one-of-a-kind resting place?

Try to write a best-of list for Rhode Islanders to embrace without including Swan Point Cemetery and you'll likely be unsuccessful. Established in 1846, it's one of the nation's oldest garden cemeteries, and its 200 acres of meticulously maintained landscape—it's also the largest greenspace contained within city limits—are filled with beautiful lawns, towering trees, floral wonder, and small waterways. Though its rather stoic entrance might hide its true nature, its billing as "picturesque and serene" rings quite true. The cemetery is known as the first choice in the city for a quiet walk or reading spot, and visitors are encouraged to spend as much time here as they would like. Its long-held reputation as the state's most prestigious cemetery stems from the great number of prominent Rhode Islanders buried here—more governors, senators, and congressmen than in any other cemetery in the state. The list includes 23 governors and such notables as famed horror fiction writer H. P. Lovecraft. The cemetery is listed on the National Register of Historic Places and is still open for new interments.

Running parallel to the cemetery's entrance, Blackstone Boulevard is a gorgeous stretch of urban greenery for a walk, bike ride, or jog.

Beautiful Swan Point Cemetery is the final resting place of some of the city's most prominent former residents. Photo courtesy of Kenneth C. Zirkel via Wikimedia Commons

SWAN POINT CEMETERY

WHAT One of the country's first garden cemeteries and the final resting place of several former governors and other prominent Rhode Islanders

WHERE 585 Blackstone Blvd., Providence

COST None

74 NARRAGANSETT RUNE STONE

What's the story behind a two-ton stone with some mysterious scribbles?

It's been called the "greatest [local] story never told," but, in fact, many people have told the story of the Narragansett Rune Stone, a rather mysterious two-and-a-half-ton slab of metasandstone with two lines of inscription that are so far of unknown origin or meaning. By most accepted accounts, the rock was discovered by a quahogger (clam digger) in 1984 near Pojac Point (overlooking Greenwich Bay in North Kingstown); photographic evidence examined after the reported finding shows the stone upland around 1939. Since it was reported to the Rhode Island Historical Preservation & Heritage Commission, many have tried to decipher how old the stone is, in what language the inscription is written, and what the words mean. Numerous experts have studied it, and several reports have concluded that the inscription matches ancient runic, or pre-Latin alphabet, characters. Some have said the inscription is Nordic, some Icelandic. One man even claimed that he carved the inscription in 1964. None of this can be confirmed, however, as no one has been able to conclusively date the stone, which would be required first. Throughout all efforts to identify the stone's origin, one

---

Wickford Village is one of the quaintest and most beautiful in the state, offering several charming day trips.

Wickford Village in North Kingstown is now home to the Narragansett Rune Stone, a two-and-a-half-ton metasandstone boulder with two lines of inscription that some say is in an ancient pre-Latin alphabet.

NARRAGANSETT RUNE STONE

WHAT Two-and-a-half-ton rock of unknown origin with an inscription that is thought to be in ancient runic characters

WHERE 55 Brown St., Wickford

COST None

sentiment has remained: Rhode Islanders are adamant that this stone is of great significance and were aghast when it went missing in 2012. It was recovered a year later. A Pojac Point resident who was so upset by so many people seeking out the stone and descending upon his neighborhood had removed the stone—one mystery solved. In 2015, the seven-foot-long, five-foot-high stone was placed with much fanfare at its current home in Old Library Park, in the Wickford village of North Kingstown, near the town hall's annex building.

75 COFFEE MILK

What's up with Rhode Island's favorite caffeinated drink?

When ordering this Rhode Island-brewed beverage, be sure to pronounce it properly—its "kaw-fee" milk—or you'll give away your tourist or transplant resident status. Rhode Island's state beverage, coffee milk is a beverage sweetened with a coffee syrup that is prepared by straining water and sugar through coffee grounds. Sound appetizing? This is one of those don't-knock-it-till-you-try-it local delicacies that is at the same time delicious and intriguing. Historians debate when the beverage was invented, but most point to the 19th-century Italian immigration surge in Providence. The state named it the official beverage in 1993, when it bested another local favorite, Del's Lemonade, in a contest. Several companies produce packaged syrup that you can pick up in stores across the state to make coffee milk at home. The syrup has been used in other popular beverages, including a limited edition "coffee milk stout" produced by Narragansett Brewery, and the "coffee cabinet," which features coffee ice cream.

For a city-centric coffee milk, visit Dave's Coffee at 341 South Main Street.

COFFEE MILK

WHAT Rhode Island State Drink made by mixing coffee syrup and milk

WHERE Various locations throughout the state

COST Depends on the restaurant

Autocrat Coffee Syrup allows you to make your own coffee milk—Rhode Island's official state beverage—at home.

165

76 BIRTH OF THE AMERICAN DINER

Which Rhode Islander invented one of America's most beloved dining traditions?

Across the United States, the diner is a beloved American institution as iconic and synonymous with all things Americana as baseball and apple pie. And its origins were no less so—a remarkable example of the entrepreneurial foundations and everyone-can-make-it spirit upon which the country prides itself. That it was a Rhode Islander whose free thinking led to this dining revolution that continues to inspire some 145 years later is still a local point of delight. In 1872, Walter Scott—who had been selling sandwiches, coffee, and snacks on the street—opened his own mobile food business from a horse-drawn wagon downtown, modifying the business model of successful, stall-based street vendors. In doing so, he was able to move locations—much the way today's food trucks do—and his style caught on across the border in Massachusetts, where, in 1887, Thomas Buckley became the first entrepreneur to form a dining car company. From there, stationary cars became the norm to accommodate congested streets as automobiles grew in popularity. Scott died in 1924, but his pioneering legacy lives on here and across the country. In Providence, two dining car must-visits are Haven Bros., a true mobile food car that appears downtown nightly and caters to late-night revelers on Dorrance Street next to City Hall, and Pawtucket's Modern Diner, a family-friendly weekend tradition.

Haven Bros. Diner provides a late-night snack fix for those out and about past dark. Photo courtesy of Swampyank via Wikimedia Commons

THE DINER

WHAT A beloved American tradition invented by Rhode Islander Walter Scott

WHERE Several locations across the state

COST Varied

The custard French toast at Pawtucket's Modern Diner was named the number 1 diner dish in America by the Food Network in 2015.

77 GREEN ANIMALS TOPIARY GARDEN

Rhode Island certainly didn't invent topiary—the art of training perennial plants to develop and maintain shapes through masterful pruning dates to Roman times—but the oldest garden in the United States exhibiting this type of living sculpture thrives in the state's historic town of Portsmouth. The estate's story started with its 1872 purchase as a summer retreat by cotton manufacturing executive Thomas E. Brayton, who hired gardener Joseph Carreiro. Starting in 1912, Carreiro began creating his topiaries, and the tradition flourished when a new generation came in, both under new ownership—by Brayton's daughter Alice—and under new care—by Carreiro's son-in-law. Today's result—an impressive collection that includes 80 sculptured trees—took decades to achieve. Visitors are awed by teddy bears, a giraffe, a reindeer, and many, many more topiary animals. The seven-acre estate also boasts 35 formal flowerbeds and vegetable and herb gardens, among other features. It was Alice Brayton who renamed the estate "Green Animals" and oversaw it during Jacqueline Bouvier's coming-out party in the late 1940s. Upon Alice's death, the garden was bequeathed to The Preservation Society of Newport County, which maintains it and oversees an annual children's party that regularly attracts large crowds eager to explore this local treasure that's often seen as a hidden gem.

The Green Animals Topiary Garden in Portsmouth is a fascinating work of art, kept alive by The Preservation Society of Newport County.

GREEN ANIMALS TOPIARY GARDEN

WHAT The oldest—and most northern—topiary garden in the United States

WHERE 380 Corys Ln., Portsmouth

COST Adults, $17.50; children ages 17 and under, $8

The garden is open seasonally—approximately mid-May through the end of October—but several other Preservation Society of Newport County properties, including some of the city's famed mansions, can be visited during the winter months. Visitors shouldn't miss the estate's 1850 Victorian Brayton House Museum, which houses a small collection of vintage toys.

78 SOUTHEAST LIGHT

Is this lighthouse, which is admired for its unique architecture, Block Island's most beautiful spot?

Block Island, situated 13 miles south of the Rhode Island mainland, from which it is separated by Block Island Sound, is one of the state's most beautiful resources. A haven for day trippers and vacationers, it has a vast amount of undeveloped land—about 40 percent of the island is designated for conservation—and it's one of only 12 Western Hemisphere spots to be named one of The Nature Conservancy's "Last Great Places." Its less than 10 square miles of land offer many stunning views, one of—if not THE—most striking is looking out from Southeast Light on the southern tip of Mohegan Bluffs, the island's clay cliffs. The lighthouse was first lit on February 1, 1875, and was designed in Gothic Revival style, which was a bit of a departure from the era's tendency to favor function over form. As such, it's considered one of the country's most sophisticated lighthouses from the 19th century. Marked features include a brick exterior and porches on the connectors to the keeper's house, which has only been altered to include modern plumbing and repair storm damage since it was originally constructed. A point of fascination with the lighthouse is that the entire 2,000-ton building was moved inland about 300 feet in 1993 because

---

SOUTHEAST LIGHT

WHAT A 19th-century lighthouse, noted for its sophisticated architecture, that once was moved in its entirety to protect it from coastal erosion

WHERE 122 Mohegan Trail, New Shoreham

COST Adults, $10; children & seniors, $5

The Southeast Lighthouse on Block Island was once moved in its entirety to get it away from an eroding shoreline.

coastal erosion threatened to cause it to fall into the sea. Many remark that the lighthouse's tower appears short for its function; insiders report this is because the tower, at 67 feet, stands at such a high elevation on Mohegan Bluffs that it can be seen more than 200 feet above water level. The Southeast Lighthouse Foundation took ownership of Southeast Light in 1992 and offers seasonal tours in addition to maintaining a small museum and gift shop at the site.

The best time to visit Block Island is during June and September, when a decent number of restaurants and shops are open for the season, but crowds are not in full force.

79 BROWN & HOPKINS COUNTRY STORE

Where in Rhode Island is the country's oldest continually operating country store?

Another Blackstone Valley gem, the Brown & Hopkins Country Store is a peach of a shopping destination in the village of Chepachet in Glocester, Rhode Island. It's treasured by locals and those who happen upon it while taking in nearby sites and dining. What many of these folks don't know is that it's the country's oldest continually operating country store. The building was constructed in 1799, and in 1809 Ira Evans opened shop with his general store. Several changes in ownership took place up through 1921, when the business was purchased by James L. Brown and William W. Hopkins. The duo renamed the store and ran it until 1964. Its current owner has been the proprietor since 2004, and though the store's stock selection has changed a bit since its founding—today it bills itself as "specializing in primitive and country home accessories," among other items—there are several reminders of the past, including a (nonworking) potbelly stove, wooden floors, beamed ceilings, and "nostalgic" penny candies displayed in an old-fashioned candy case. A recent addition is the shop's custom farm tables and furniture, which are made in New England on order.

Brown & Hopkins Country Store in the quiet village of Chepatchet is the country's oldest general store, established in 1809.

BROWN & HOPKINS COUNTRY STORE

WHAT Country's oldest, continually operating country store

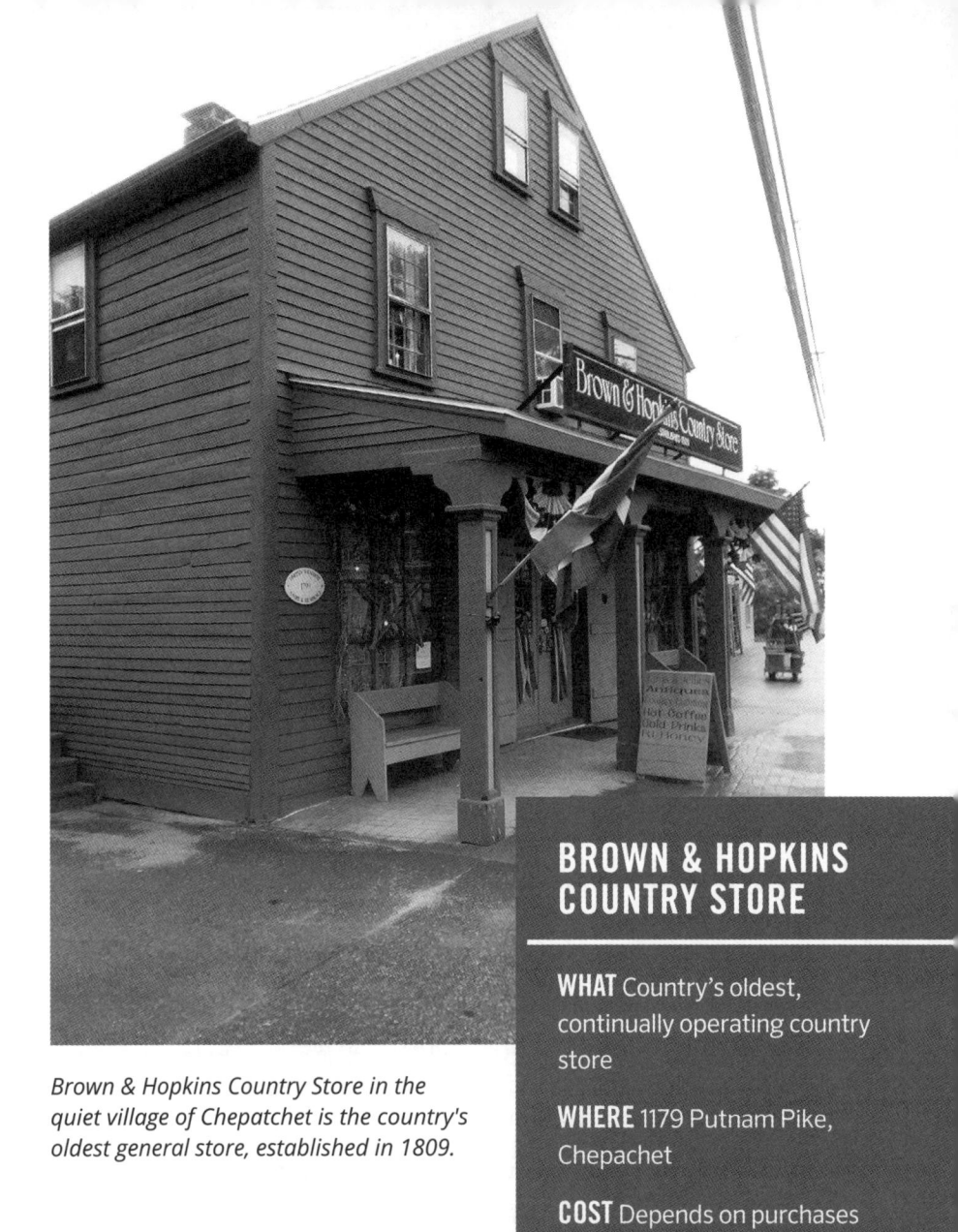

WHERE 1179 Putnam Pike, Chepachet

COST Depends on purchases

Nearby is the Purple Cat Vineyard & Winery, one of the state's newest vino additions, worth a visit for its stunning merlot.

173

80 NEWPORT TOWER

Is this city-by-the-sea landmark the remains of a stone windmill or evidence of precolonial life in Rhode Island?

Newport Tower in the city's Touro Park is well known as a historical landmark but perhaps even better known for the many theories surrounding its origin. At the center of the debate is the fact that no one really knows who actually built the tower, when they did it, or what its intended use was. In his 1677 will, Benedict Arnold—not THAT Mr. Arnold but his great-grandfather, Rhode Island's first Colonial governor—noted that the tower standing behind his now-demolished mansion was his stone-built windmill. While this has satisfied many—the conclusion that Arnold built it and that it was, at least for a time, used as a windmill—that hasn't stopped many others from theorizing that it was a mark left by Nordic conquerors, medieval Scottish knights, or Chinese explorers, or that it was built by Native Americans before colonization. Many investigations of these theories have mentioned Colonial-era documents indicating that the tower was standing when colonists arrived here. Its physical appearance is similar to European churches from the 1100s, and its structural characteristics indicate possible use as an observatory, such as those that 13th-century Chinese sailors used. A 2003 report on carbon dating conducted in the early 1990s put construction at approximately 1680, suggesting that the tower Arnold mentioned in his will is not the one that stands today and that it is likely a reconstructed version.

Debate still surrounds the origins of the Newport Tower, thought to have once been a working windmill. Photo courtesy of Swampyank via Wikimedia Commons

NEWPORT TOWER

WHAT 17th-century windmill rumored—and refuted—to be have been built by Nordic conquerors or other precolumbian North American visitors

WHERE 5 Touro Park St. West, Newport

COST None

Mystery lovers may consider a night view of the tower, when it is illuminated by ground lighting that provides an eerie glow.

81 H. P. LOVECRAFT

How did this relatively obscure author have immense posthumous popularity?

Rhode Islanders—particularly the literary circle of Providence—are proud of H. P. Lovecraft, a 20th-century author of horror fiction who lived most of his life in their capital city. His legacy is undeniable—some fandom followers seem to be obsessed—and his influence is marked, with modern-day creations referencing or incorporating his ideals and published works in genres from fiction (Stephen King) to television (*Babylon 5*) and music (Metallica). Philosophers and biographers have studied him, and festivals are held in his honor, but during his lifetime, Howard Phillips Lovecraft was an unknown, struggling artist, and by several accounts a sickly and strange individual. He was born in August 1890 on Angell Street in Providence and was raised largely by his mother after his father was committed to Butler Hospital, a psychiatric hospital that still operates today. It's said that as an adult he had a rather pale complexion due to his preference to remain indoors during daylight hours. He had some early creative success through the United Amateur Press Association and was remarkably dogged in his pursuit of creative expression even though he never enjoyed financial success. In his later years, he repeatedly had to move to accommodate a dwindling bank account, and it is said he was sometimes starving in his effort to keep up with his network of correspondence that included *Psycho* author Robert Bloch. What is it about a writer who achieved no widespread recognition in his lifetime that has so enthralled fans since his death in 1937 at age 47? In short order, it's his writing and the public's tendency only to fully embrace creative genius after the creator is no longer with us. Rhode Islanders have always welcomed

H. P. Lovecraft, who lived in relative obscurity during his life, is now seen as the father of weird fiction. His work continues to influence modern genre authors. Photo courtesy of Kenneth C. Zirkel via Wikimedia Commons

H. P. LOVECRAFT

WHAT Providence author who rose to fame largely after his death and is known as one of the 20th century's most prominent authors of horror fiction

WHERE Lovecraft's grave site is in Swan Point Cemetery, 585 Blackstone Blvd., Providence

COST None

the unusual and rebellious. The fact that Lovecraft's stories and novellas are laced with references to Providence and city locations probably doesn't hurt.

Another spot to pay tribute to Lovecraft is H.P. Lovecraft Memorial Square, named by the city of Providence in 2013 at the intersection of Angell and Prospect Streets. The square stands near Lovecraft's former homes.

82 LITTLE BET

Why does Rhode Island have a tribute to a fallen circus elephant?

This is not a happy story. In the 1800s, Hachaliah Bailey—a distant relation to Bailey Circus founder James Bailey, who later would go on to merge talents and form the recently closed Ringling Bros. and Barnum & Bailey Circus—became one of the first traveling circus owners to use an elephant in his show. By today's standards, he would not be judged a particularly ethical man. When his first elephant, Old Bet, was shot and killed by religious New Englanders who did not care for the fanfare she brought with her, he simply bought another elephant. Little Bet, official named Betty the Fabulous Learned Elephant, was an attraction up and down the East Coast in the 1820s until one fateful spring evening in 1826. After finishing a show in Chepachet, Rhode Island, Little Bet met the same demise as her predecessor. Seven men from the local order of Masons were named responsible for shooting Little Bet as she crossed a bridge and were ousted from their order. Not much more attention was paid to the crime for another 150 years, when the town's historian led an effort to claim May 25, 1976, as "Elephant Day" and dedicate a plaque in honor of their fallen elephant.

> MAY 25, 1826 — MAY 25, 1976
> DIVERSE HANDS FIRED UPON
> **BETTY**
> ONE OF AMERICA'S FIRST ELEPHANTS
> AT THE NORTH END OF THE
> RUSTIC SPAN THAT ARCHED
> CHEPACHET RIVER
>
> GIVEN IN OBSERVATION OF THE
> 150TH ANNIVERSARY OF THE EVENT BY
> RICHMOND AND EDNA KENT

Chepatchet residents dedicated a plaque in honor of Little Bet, a traveling entertainment elephant who was shot down by locals in the 1820s.

LITTLE BET PLAQUE

WHAT Commemorative plaque dedicated to the memory of "Little Bet," a show elephant who was gunned down by local Masons in 1826

WHERE Route 44, north of Douglas Hook Rd., Chepachet

COST None

Behind Chepachet town hall, there is a Mr. Potato Head Statue—once part of a statewide tourism effort—designed as an ode to Little Bet.

83 RHODE ISLAND'S PLYMOUTH ROCK

Rhode Island and neighboring Massachusetts have always had a bit of a rivalry. Sure, we root for the same sports teams, but we constantly debate over nearly everything else, from which state houses the best educational facilities (Harvard vs. Brown) to which capital city has the best Italian food (the North End vs. Federal Hill). Some point to the circumstances surrounding Rhode Island's founding as the rivalry's origin—when Rhode Island founder Roger Williams fled Plymouth County, Massachusetts, to escape religious prosecution and persecution. So, it makes sense that Rhode Islanders wanted to commemorate his rumored landing rock in similar fashion to the historic Plymouth Rock. The only trouble was that the slate rock was accidentally blown to shreds when city workers were trying to recover it (the rock had become embedded in shore land) as part of the state's project to mark the spot in 1906. So, a planned pavilion at the landing spot on the Seekonk River was scrapped, and instead the city erected a monument on the spot, which is now called Slate Rock Park but is also known as What Cheer Square or Roger Williams Square. It should be noted that Williams's actual landing spot is still debated, as historical records about the event don't really exist, and some insist the conclusion that it happened at Slate Rock Park is rather dubious.

Rhode Island founder Roger Williams is said to have landed at what is now Slate Rock Park, and a monument was erected to commemorate the spot in the early 1900s.

ROGER WILLIAMS LANDING PLACE

WHAT Monument erected at the site thought to be where state founder Roger Williams first touched land here

WHERE Williams and Gano Sts., Providence

COST None

Pieces of "slate rock" can be found in various locations throughout the city, including in the vestibule floor of Central Baptist Church on Wayland Avenue.

84 JFK GRAVE SLAB

Where can you pay respects to a fallen president?

President John F. Kennedy's ties to Newport, Rhode Island, are well known. Victorian mansion Hammersmith Farm was where he and First Lady Jacqueline Bouvier Kennedy held their wedding reception—it was also Mrs. Kennedy's childhood home—and during Kennedy's administration, it was called the "Summer White House." Within the seaside city is also a little-known Kennedy artifact, albeit one with less celebratory association. A rejected grave marker that was designed for Kennedy's grave at Arlington National Cemetery has found its own resting spot behind the Boys & Girls Clubs of Newport County building. Back in 1965, local stone carver John Benson—who has also carved gravestones for such luminaries as Tennessee Williams and monuments including the FDR Memorial in Washington, D.C.—was asked to engrave Kennedy's famous 1961 inauguration speech into granite that would be installed at Arlington. One piece of a rejected version, in which Benson broke the speech up into five pieces, was discovered by a Boys & Girls Club worker in nearby Middletown in 1986. Only speculation has provided reasons as to how the 800-pound marker ended up at either club location—even Benson has said he doesn't know how it happened—which adds a bit of mystery to the entire affair.

A rejected version of the Arlington National Cemetery memorial for President John F. Kennedy now rests in the front yard of the Boys & Girls Club in Newport. No one seems to know how this 800-pound stone ended up here.

JFK GRAVE SLAB

WHAT Rejected submission for President JFK's grave

WHERE 95 Church St., Newport

COST None

Hammersmith Farm is privately owned and not available to the public, but St. Mary's Church at 14 William Street, the site of the Kennedys' nuptials, is nearby and is also an important piece of Newport history, since it was the first Catholic parish established in Rhode Island and sits on the National Register of Historic Places.

85 YOU'RE A GRAND OL' RHODE ISLANDER

Which high-flying native Rhode Islander helped shape Broadway as we know it today?

With the large statue dedicated to him that stands in Times Square in New York City, some may not know that George M. Cohan—penner of "You're a Grand Old Flag" and other works and subject of the film *Yankee Doodle Dandy*—was a Rhode Islander. He was born in Providence—either on July 3 (according to his birth certificate) or July 4 (according to his family)—in 1878 and was a performer by the age of eight, joining The Four Cohans family act and making his Broadway debut in an 1893 sketch. He wasn't a permanent Rhode Islander, since the family toured much of the year and summered in Massachusetts. By his teenage years, he was a published songwriter, and in 1901 he wrote, directed, and produced his first Broadway musical. He went on to have a storied and successful career. He's most well known for songs and contributions to what we today call Broadway,

---

Today's musicals that play at the Providence Performing Arts Center likely wouldn't have been possible without Cohan, so consider paying tribute to him by seeing a show there.

George M. Cohan, one of the men responsible for what we now know as Broadway tunes, was born in Rhode Island.

GEORGE M. COHAN

WHAT Native Rhode Islander, notable for his contributions to creating the book musical

WHERE N/A

COST None

since he is considered by some to have been an "early pioneer" of the book musical. His notable works include "Over There," a song most often associated with World War I. He wrote several Broadway musicals and was awarded the 1936 Congressional Gold Medal for his contributions to increase morale during the war. The honor, bestowed upon him by President Franklin Delano Roosevelt, was the first Congressional Gold Medal given to a person in an artistic field.

86 ELIZABETH ALDEN GRAVE

Is the first white girl born in New England buried in a small Rhode Island cemetery?

Elizabeth Alden Pabodie's grave marker at the Old Burying Ground (Commons Burial Ground) in Little Compton reads "Daughter of Plymouth Pilgrims John Alden & Priscilla Mullin, the first white woman born in New England....who dyed may ye 31st 1717 and in the 94th year of her age." By most accounts, this testament is true, and historians have long been fascinated that the first girl born to New England colonists—this would be 1623—is buried in a small cemetery in the center of one of Rhode Island's less visible towns.

It's thought that Elizabeth was the second white child born here, and that the first was a boy, Peregrine White, in 1620. Elizabeth's parents, John Alden and Priscilla Mullin, sailed to America on the *Mayflower* in 1620. As an adult, Elizabeth married William Pabodie, and they moved from Plymouth County, Massachusetts, to Little Compton when William became one of the first men to buy land there. Her final resting place, the Old Burying Ground in the town's common (where a church once stood), is a historically important location, since there are not that many church cemeteries here. This is because the state was founded on, essentially, a separation of church and state statute. Little Compton, however, was settled by descendants of Puritan Pilgrims, whose religious philosophy was a bit different. In fact, the town was originally part of Plymouth Colony and wasn't declared part of Rhode Island until 1746.

Elizabeth Alden is thought to have been the first girl born to American colonists. Photo courtesy of Swampyank via Wikimedia Commons

ELIZABETH ALDEN GRAVE

WHAT Burial site of the woman believed to be the first girl born to English colonists in New England

WHERE Commons Burial Ground, Commons St., Little Compton

COST None

Go around lunchtime and stop in at the Commons Lunch, a long-standing local favorite across the street.

87 WEIRD LAWS

Why might Rhode Island be the best place to survive the zombie apocalypse?

Every state across America has them—almost archaic laws that (most likely) served some purpose to keep its citizens honest and upstanding but seem downright weird today. Rhode Island is no exception, and a brief examination of some of its still-on-the-books rules and regulations is an opportunity for a good laugh. For example, it's apparently illegal to bite off another person's limb—in some accounts the law is even more specific and forbids chewing on a left leg—which would make Rhode Island the ideal place to hide out from zombies and any other flesh-eating monsters. Another doozy is that it's illegal to play athletic games on Sundays except for hockey and ice polo. Football and baseball would require a special license to hold games. It's also against the law to impersonate a town sealer, auctioneer, or fence-viewer, and an infraction is punishable by a fine of at least $20. One could understand false impersonation laws, but it's the very specific grouping—and perhaps the inclusion of fence-viewer—that leaves many shaking their heads at this law. Other weird laws include prohibiting the throwing of pickle juice on a trolley and testing a horse's speed on a highway.

Like most states, Rhode Island has some old laws that are still on the books but no longer make much sense. Photo courtesy of Xmap via Wikimedia Commons

WEIRD LAWS

WHAT Strange laws still on the books in Rhode Island

WHERE N/A

COST None

It's been long rumored that you'd face a fine for selling a toothbrush and toothpaste to the same customer on a Sunday in Rhode Island, but that supposed law isn't intact.

88 NINE MEN'S MISERY

Where in Rhode Island is the rumored oldest veterans memorial in the United States?

Not many Rhode Island communities escaped the devastation of King Philip's War, and what is now Cumberland, the state's northeasternmost town that is just minutes away from neighboring Massachusetts. For what some consider one of Rhode Island's sleepier towns, there's a sizable history here, and the most visible example of that is the Nine Men's Misery, a tomb surrounded by a stone memorial that is thought to be the nation's oldest veterans memorial. In March 1676 during what is known as Pierce's Fight, English colonist Capt. Michael Pierce led a charge to capture Narragansett Indians but failed. Nearly all fighting colonists were killed in the subsequent battle—including Capt. Pierce. Nine colonists were taken prisoner and, in what makes this fight one of the war's bloodiest, were reportedly tortured to death. Other English soldiers discovered their bodies, buried them, and surrounded the site with a group of stones in their memory. In 1928, when the land on which the memorial sits still belonged to the former Abbey of Our

---

Stop by the Cumberland Public Library to pick up a map that will take you on a 15-minute walk through the woods to the eerie monument.

This war memorial is thought to be the oldest one dedicated to veterans in the country. Photo courtesy of Arlene Nicholson, reprinted with permission from Yankee Xpress

NINE MEN'S MISERY

WHAT Site containing a stone memorial believed to be the oldest veterans memorial in the United States

WHERE 1464 Diamond Hill Rd., Cumberland (library)

COST None

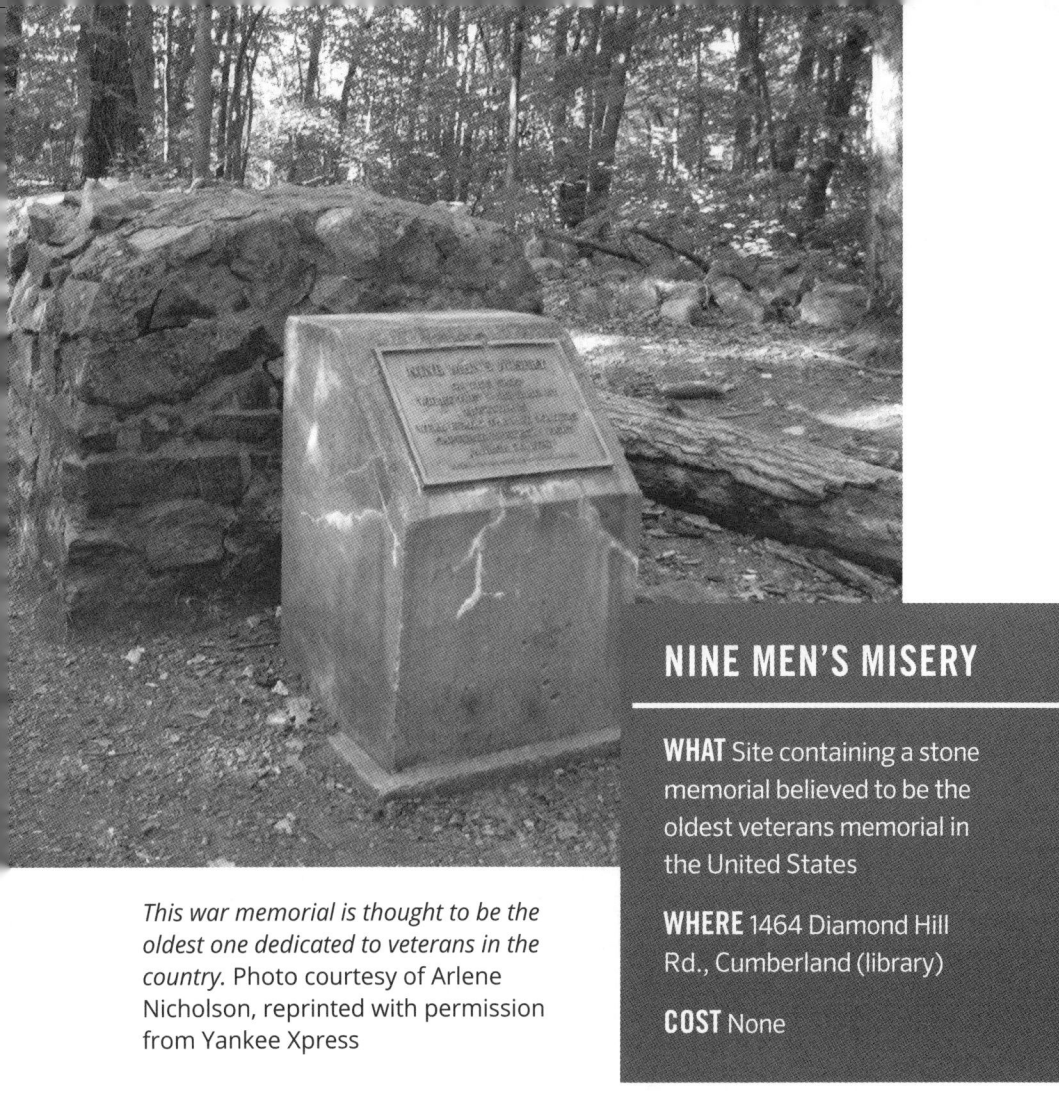

Lady of the Valley Trappist monastery, monks who resided there built a landmark to commemorate the site and stop periodic desecrations of and disturbances to the memorial. The stone is inscribed: "On this spot, where they were slain by the Indians, were buried the nine soldiers captured in Pierce's Fight, March 26, 1676." The area is regularly described as one of the eeriest in the state—with reports of ghosts of those who were tortured roaming the site.

89 TENNIS, ANYONE?

Where can you celebrate the birthplace of American tennis?

Did you know that the first U.S. National Championship tennis tournament took place in Rhode Island, more specifically, at the site of what is now the International Tennis Hall of Fame in Newport, Rhode Island, from August 31 to September 3, 1881? It's one of the more unknown Rhode Island firsts and an extraordinary one, considering the history of tennis that has unfolded since that time. The 1881 games took place at the Newport Casino, which was built in 1880 as a social club for Newport's summer elite and housed the U.S. Lawn Tennis Association championships through 1914. When casino president Jimmy Van Alen toured the National Baseball Hall of Fame in the 1950s, he became inspired to establish a similar tribute to the game of tennis and established the museum in 1954. It's been recognized by the International Tennis Federation since 1986. Today, the museum displays about 2,000 objects in "highly interactive" exhibits and showcases. Exhibits are organized chronologically, taking visitors through the history of tennis from its origins to the game as it is known today. Dedicated to preserving and promoting the history of tennis, the museum also hosts events in the building's historic Casino Theatre, which is noted for its decorative, gold-trimmed ivory interior and has a seating capacity of 500.

The International Tennis Hall of Fame is known as the birthplace of American tennis. Photo courtesy of John Phalen via Wikimedia Commons

INTERNATIONAL TENNIS HALL OF FAME

WHAT Museum promoting the history of tennis at the site of the former Newport Casino, a turn-of-the-century social club for Newport's elite

WHERE 194 Bellevue Ave., Newport

COST Adults, $15; seniors, members, and students, $12; children ages 16 and under, free

If you're a player, be sure to stop by the pro shop, which sells top-notch tools of the trade.

90 STUCK IN A GUN

Where can you see a muzzled cannon used by Rhode Islanders who fought in the Civil War?

Battery B, 1st Regiment Rhode Island Light Artillery saw a remarkable amount of action during the Civil War and is well known for its heroic, though perhaps unintentional, efforts to defeat Southern forces at the Battle of Gettysburg on July 3, 1863. On the third day of battle, the artillery's 12-pound Napoleon cannon was struck by a Confederate gun and exploded, killing two artillery members and leaving it severely damaged. When other regiment members tried to load it for retaliatory fire, the charge would not properly load and became stuck so that the gun was no longer operable. Because the Confederates knew that the Union army's manpower and arsenal of weapons were depleted, the cannon incident contributed to their decision that the time for Pickett's Charge had come. This assault proved to be devastating to the Confederates and is considered a turning point in the war, from which the South never recovered. The Gettysburg Gun, as the cannon came to be known, was returned to Rhode Island in 1874 and has been on display here since then, except for two days in August 1962 when the Rhode Island National Guard had to remove

---

Free guided tours of the State House are offered five times daily—at 9:00 a.m., 10:00 a.m., 11:00 a.m., 1:00 p.m., and 2:00 p.m. Reservations are only required for groups of 10 or more.

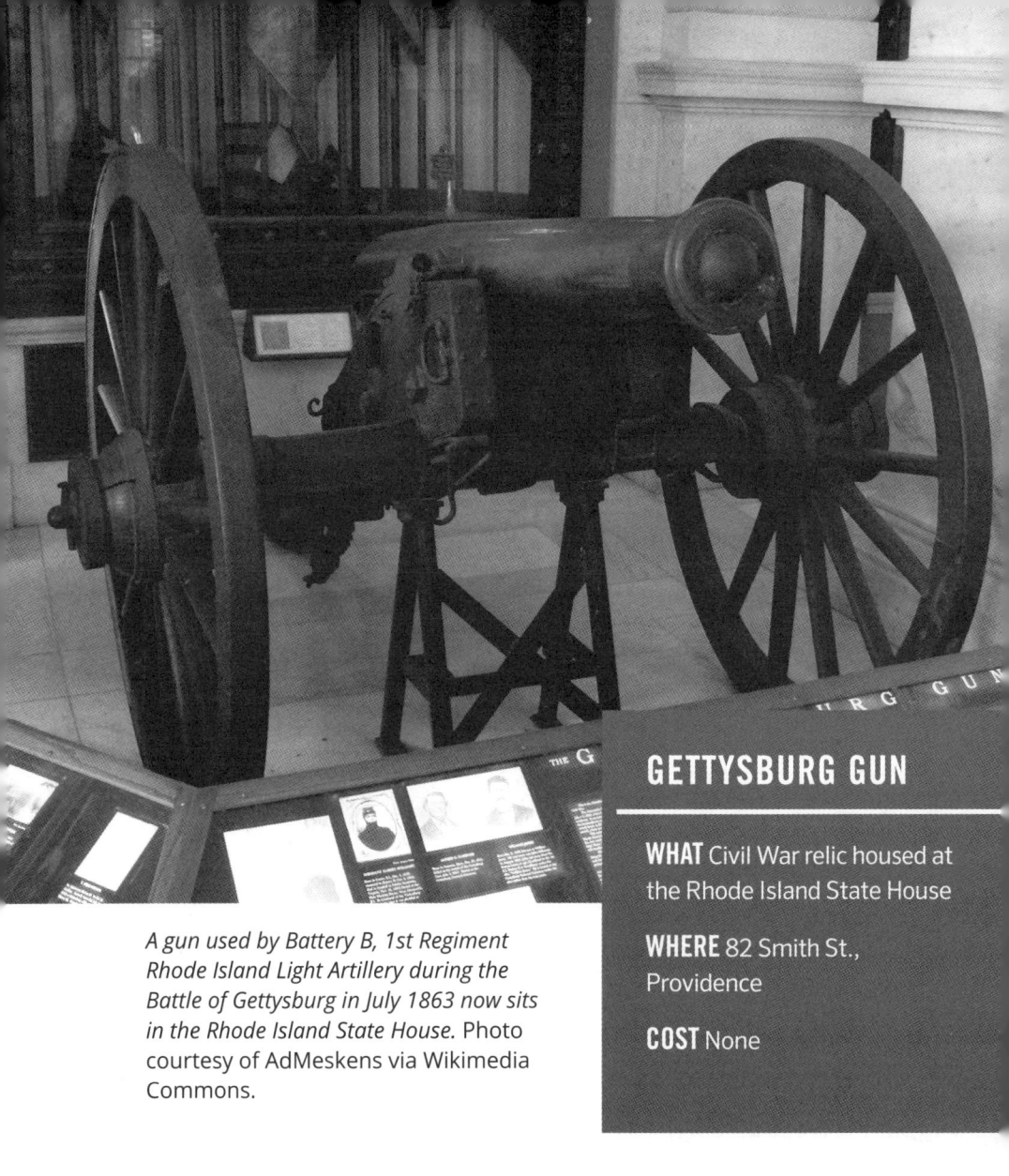

A gun used by Battery B, 1st Regiment Rhode Island Light Artillery during the Battle of Gettysburg in July 1863 now sits in the Rhode Island State House. Photo courtesy of AdMeskens via Wikimedia Commons.

GETTYSBURG GUN

WHAT Civil War relic housed at the Rhode Island State House

WHERE 82 Smith St., Providence

COST None

two-and-a-half pounds. of black gunpowder from the cannon. Since gunpower becomes more sensitive with age, it was feared the gun could explode. The cannon is housed at the Rhode Island State House in the foyer of the building's main public entrance, available to see for all interested in this unique piece of state history.

INDEX

Abbey of Our Lady of the Valley Trappist Monastery, 191
Adamsville, Rhode Island, 12, 13
Allie's Donuts, 18
American Industrial Revolution, 24, 26, 70, 71
American Revolution, 38, 52, 56, 136, 148
America's Cup, 149
Angell Street, 176
Arcade Building, 139
Arts and Crafts movement, 86, 87
Audrain Automobile Museum, 44, 45
Audubon Society of Rhode Island, 12
Aurora Civic Association, 159
Avery, The, 67
Bajnotti, Paul, 150
Bajnotti, Carrie Mathilde Brown, 150, 151
Ballou graveyard, 156, 157
Bally, Boris, 4, 5
Barnaby, Jerothmul, 36
Barnaby's Castle, 36, 37, 102
Baseball Hall of Fame, 16, 192
Battle of Gettysburg, 194, 195
Battle of San Juan Hill, 148
Benefit Street, 52, 53
Big Blue Bug Solutions, 2, 3
Big Nazo, 76, 77
Bizarre Foods with Andrew Zimmern, 28
Blackstone, William, 24
Blackstone Boulevard, 160, 161, 177
Blackstone River, 24
Blackstone Valley Tourism Council, 24, 25, 40, 41, 71
Block Island, 112, 113, 170, 171
Blue violet, 152, 153
Borden, Lizzie, 48, 49
Boys & Girls Clubs of Newport County, 182, 183
Bradley, Edson, 146

Bristol, Rhode Island, 42, 43, 83, 134, 135
Bristol Fourth of July Parade, 134, 135
Broadway Street, 37, 159, 184, 185
Brown & Hopkins Country Store, 172, 173
Brown, Mercy, 46, 47
Brown, Nicholas, Jr., 150, 151
Brown University, 6, 7, 60, 150, 151, 154
Burke, Robert, 150
Burleigh, Sydney Richmond, 86
Burnside, Ambrose, 8, 9
Burnside Park, 8, 9, 150, 151
Burriville, 62, 63
Calamari, 158, 159
Camille's, 66, 67
Carey Mansion, 146, 147
Carreiro, Joseph, 168
Carrie Brown Bajnotti Memorial Fountain, 150
Carrie Tower, 150
Central Baptist Church, 181
Central Falls, 25, 72, 73
Charlestown, Rhode Island, 54, 55
Chepachet, 82, 172, 173, 178, 179
Chief Metacomet, 110
Chief Sachem, 110
Child, Julia, 150
Chinese Dragon Boat Races, 40, 41
Civil War, 8, 142, 194, 195
Cliffside Inn, 117
Coffee milk, 158, 164, 165
Cogswell, Caroline, 72
Cogswell Tower, 72, 73
Cohan, George M., 184, 185
College Hill, 10, 86, 87
Commons Burial Ground, 186, 187
Commons Lunch, 187
Conanicut Island, 148
Crook Point Bascule Bridge, 58, 59
Cumberland, 27, 156, 157, 190, 191
Cumberlandite, 156, 157

Dark Shadows, 146, 147
Dave's Coffee, 164
Davisville, Rhode Island, 74
Declaration of Independence, 154, 155
Del's Lemonade, 164
Doran, Mary, 124
Dorrance Street, 166
Doyle, Thomas, 84
Duke, Doris, 44
Dunkin' Donuts, 18, 82
East Side, 15, 19, 87
Elephant Day, 178
Exeter, Rhode Island, 47, 129
Exeter, 128, 129
Fall River, Massachusetts, 48, 49
Family Guy, 20, 28
Fantastic Umbrella Factory, 54, 55
Farewell Street, 114
Federal Hill, 66, 67, 180
Ferron, Rose, 130, 131
First Continental Congress, 154
First Rhode Island Militia, 56
First Unitarian Church, 118, 119
Fleur-de-Lys Studios, 86, 87
Flying Horse Carousel, 68, 69
Fort Adams, 142, 143
Fort Hamilton Barracks, 38
Fort Wetherill, 148, 149
Foster, Rhode Island, 60
Gaggers, 28, 30, 31
Gano Street, 59, 181
Gettysburg Gun, 194, 195
Ghost Hunters, 84
Glendale, Rhode Island, 62, 63
Glocester, Rhode Island, 172
Graves, Thomas Thatcher, Dr., 36
Great Swamp Fight Monument, 110, 111
Green Animals Topiary Garden, 105, 168, 169
Gun Totem, 4, 5
H. P. Lovecraft Memorial Square, 177
Hachiko, 34, 35
Hammersmith Farm, 182, 183
Harris, Abigail, 52, 53
Harrison, Peter, 136

Hasbro, 82
Haven Bros., 166, 167
Hemenway's, 159
Highpointing, 60
Hirsh, Michael, Dr., 4
Hope High School, 33
Hope Street, 14, 15, 33
Hopkins, Stephen, 154, 155
Hopkintown, Rhode Island, 56
Hot wiener, 30, 31
Hurricane Carol, 108
Industrial Trust Building, 20, 21
International Tennis Hall of Fame, 192, 193
Irish, George, Col., 56
Irish Lot, 56, 57
J. B. Barnaby & Co., 36
Jailhouse Inn, 106, 107
Jamestown, Rhode Island, 148, 149
Jenks Park, 72
Jerimoth Hill, 60, 61
JFK grave slab, 182, 183
John Brown House Museum, 10, 11
John Hay Library, 6
Johnny cakes, 78, 79
Johnston, Rhode Island, 120, 121
Justine's, 67
Kennedy, Jacqueline Bouvier, 168, 180, 182
Kennedy, John F., 182, 183
Kennedy Plaza, 8, 9
Kenyon's Grist Mill, 78, 79
King Philip's War, 72, 73, 110, 111, 190
Korean War, 74
Ladd School, 128, 129
Legion Memorial Drive, 123
Life magazine, 116
Little Bet, 82, 178, 179
Little Compton, Rhode Island, 12, 186, 187
Lovecraft, H. P., 52, 53, 76, 86, 138, 139, 160, 176, 177
Lovecraft Arts & Sciences Council, 138, 139
Luongo Square, 67
MacFarlane, Seth, 20, 28
Mad Peck, 14

Massachusetts Wampanoag, 110
Mayflower, 186
McCoy Stadium, 16, 17
Middletown, Rhode Island, 56, 57, 126, 127, 182
Modern Diner, 166, 167
Mohegan Bluffs, 112, 113, 170, 171
Mr. Potato Head, 82, 83, 179
Musée Patamécanique, 42, 43
Museum of Work and Culture, 80, 81
Narragansett Bay, 38, 39, 149, 156
Narragansett Brewery, 23
Narragansett Rune Stone, 162, 163
Narragansett Tribe, 110, 122, 140
National Historic Landmark, 68, 69, 70, 142
National Register of Historic Places, 12, 13, 38, 50, 69, 72, 108, 160, 183
Nature Conservancy, The, 170
NecronomiCon Providence, 76, 89, 138, 139
Neutaconkanut Hill, 122, 123
New Brick Church, 118
New Shoreham, Rhode Island, 170
Newport, Rhode Island, 38, 39, 44, 45, 56, 65, 106, 107, 114, 115, 116, 117, 132, 136, 137, 142, 143, 146, 147, 149, 168, 169, 174, 175, 182, 183, 192, 193
Newport Bridge, 38, 143
Newport Casino, 192, 193
Newport Colony General Assembly, 14, 132
Newport Common Burying Ground, 65
Newport County Assembly, 56
Newport Harbor, 143
Newport Police Department, 106
Newport Tower, 174, 175
Nibbles Woodaway, 2, 3
Nichols, Jonathan, 114
Nincheri, Guido, 26
Nine Men's Misery, 190, 191
North End, 118, 180
North Kingstown, Rhode Island, 18, 74, 75, 162, 163

Olneyville, Rhode Island, 30, 31, 122
Olneyville New York System, 30, 31
Olneyville Square, 67
Pabodie, Elizabeth Alden, 186, 187
Palatine Light, The, 112, 113
Pawtucket, Rhode Island, 16, 17, 40, 41, 70, 71, 82, 83, 166, 167
Pawtucket Red Sox, 16
Pickett's Charge, 194
Pierce, Michael, Capt., 72, 190
Pierce's Fight, 72, 190, 191
Pinque, Erminio, 76
Plymouth Colony, 186
Plymouth County, 180, 186
Portsmouth, Rhode Island, 144, 145, 168, 169
Portsmouth Historical Society, 144
Precious Blood Cemetery, 130, 131
Preservation Society of Newport County, The, 114, 168, 169
Price, Bruce, 44
Princess Augusta, 112, 113
Prohibition, 66, 67, 109
Prospect Street, 7, 177
Prospect Terrace Park, 10
Providence Biltmore Hotel, 108, 109
Providence City Archives, 84
Providence City Hall, 84, 85, 166
Providence Federal Building and U.S. Courthouse, 4, 5
Providence Flea, The, 32, 33
Providence Journal Company, 12
Providence motto, 23
Providence Parks Department, 4
Providence Performing Arts Center, 50, 51, 184
Providence Preservation Society, 21
Providence Public Library, 86
Providence River Greenway, 33
Purgatory Avenue, 126
Purgatory Chasm, 99, 126, 127
Purple Cat Vineyard & Winery, 173
PVDonuts, 18, 19
Quahog, 28, 29, 158, 162
Quahogging, 28

Quahog Week, 29
Redwood Library, 136
Revere, Paul, 118, 119
Revere Bell, 88, 118, 119
Rhode Island arms of the state, 14
Rhode Island Cherry Blossom Festival, 34
Rhode Island Chinese Dragon Boat Races & Taiwan Day Festival, 40, 41
Rhode Island Department of Environmental Management, 29
Rhode Island Federation of Garden Clubs, 12
Rhode Island General Assembly, 14, 114, 132
Rhode Island Historical Society, 10, 11
Rhode Island Monthly, 150
Rhode Island motto, 14
Rhode Island National Guard, 194
Rhode Island Red Club of America, 12
Rhode Island School of Design, 42, 76
Rhode Island State House, 1, 64, 65, 78, 194, 195
Rhode Island State Legislature, 64, 158
Rhode Island Supreme Court, 154, 155
Rhode Island Wild Plant Society, 152
Roberts, Dennis J., 12
Rochester Red Wings, 16
Roger Williams Landing Place, 181
Roger Williams Park, 140, 141, 150, 151
Roger Williams Park Botanical Center, 140
Roger Williams Park Museum of Natural History and Planetarium, 26
Roger Williams Park Zoo, 140
Rose Ferron Foundation of Rhode Island, 130
Rose Island, 38
Rose Island Lighthouse, 38, 39, 104
Rose Island Lighthouse Foundation, 38, 39
Salley, Neil, 42, 43
Salve Regina University, 146
Samuel Slater, 24, 25
Scherzer Rolling Lift Bridge Company, 58
Seabee motto, 75
Seabee Museum & Memorial Park, 74, 75
Seekonk River, 22, 59, 180
Sideburns, 8, 9
Silver Lake, 122
Slater, Samuel, 70
Slater Mill, 70, 71
Slater Mill Historic Site, 70, 71
Snake Den Farm, 120
Snake Den State Park, 120
South Beach, 126
South Main Street, 81, 159, 164
Southeast Light, 170, 171
Spanish-American War, 142, 148
Spring Lake Arcade, 62, 63
St. Anne's Cultural Center, 26, 27
St. Mary's Catholic Church, 124, 125
St. Mary's Church, Newport, 183
Stephen Harris House, 52, 53
Stuart, Gilbert, 64, 65
Stuffies, 28, 29
Superman, 20, 21
Swan Point Cemetery, 8, 85, 160, 161, 177
Swift, Taylor, 68
Tall Ships America, 149
Temple to Music, 140, 141
Thomas Street, 87
Touro, Isaac, 136
Touro Synagogue, 96, 136, 137
Tuckerman Avenue, 126, 127
Turner, Beatrice, 116, 117
U.S. Army, 142, 143, 146
U.S. Library of Congress, 86
U.S. Navy, 74, 75, 142
Union Station, 58, 59

199

V-J Day, 132, 133
Vietnam, 74
War of 1812, 142
Warren, Rhode Island, 82
Warwick, Rhode Island, 153
Washington, George, 56, 64, 65, 137, 155
Watch Hill, 68, 69
Westminster Street, 21, 77
West Warwick, Rhode Island, 26, 125
West Kingston, Rhode Island, 79, 111
West Side, 36
Westerly, Rhode Island, 69
White Horse Tavern, 114, 115
Wicked Tulips Flower Farm, 120, 121
Wickford, Rhode Island, 162, 163
Wickford Village, Rhode Island, 162, 163
Wight, Henry, Rev., 134
Williams, Betsey, 140
Williams, Roger, 10, 11, 22, 26, 122, 140, 141, 150, 151, 180, 181
Williams Street, 59, 181
Willson, Edmund R., 86
Woonsocket, Rhode Island, 26, 27, 34, 35, 80, 81, 130, 131
Woonsocket train depot, 35
World War I, 20, 142, 148, 185
World War II, 74, 132, 133, 142, 146, 148